ACOUSTIC GUITAR

privqte lessons

TEACH YOURSELF GUITAR BASICS

By Jeffrey Pepper Rodgers and the Master Teachers at *Acoustic Guitar* Magazine

STRING LETTER PUBLISHING

Publisher: David A. Lusterman
Group Publisher and Editorial Director: Dan Gabel
Editor: Jeffrey Pepper Rodgers
Music Editor and Engraver: Andrew DuBrock
Art Director: Barbara Summer
Production Designer: Kristin Wallace

Cover Photograph: Barbara Summer

Portions of this book were previously published as *Beginning Guitarist's
    Handbook*, © 2001 String Letter Publishing

ISBN 978-1-890490-91-1

This book was produced by String Letter Publishing, Inc.
PO Box 767, San Anselmo, CA 94979-0767
(415) 485-6946; stringletter.com

Library of Congress Cataloging-in-Publication Data

Rodgers, Jeffrey Pepper, 1964-
  Teach Yourself Guitar Basics / by Jeffrey Pepper Rodgers and the Master Teachers at
Acoustic Guitar magazine.
      p. cm. – (Acoustic Guitar Private Lessons)
  Includes bibliographical references and index.
  ISBN 978-1-890490-91-1 (pbk. : alk. paper)
  1. Guitar–Methods–Self-instruction 2. Guitar–Instruction and study. I. Acoustic guitar.
II. Title.
  MT588.R635 2009
  787.87'193–dc22
                        2009048660

STRING LETTER PUBLISHING

Contents

Introduction

If you're just getting started on guitar, I'd wager that two things are true: You want to play—now. And you've got a ton of questions about how and what and where and why. This book was written to help you on both fronts.

In the opening section you'll find a six-pack of lessons to get you up and playing today—from your first chords and strums through the basics of power chords, fingerpicking, and music theory, and even your first solo. You'll find all the examples on the accompanying CD, so you can hear the sounds and grooves you're aiming for and loop them until they fall easily under your fingers. One of the beauties of the guitar is that so much of rock, country, blues, folk, and more uses these simple ingredients and nothing more—so you can make real music with only what you'll learn in these starter lessons.

The balance of *Teach Yourself Guitar Basics* is devoted to advice about instruments and gear—a source of tremendous confusion for seasoned players as well as newcomers—and the learning process. From my own experience as a player, to more than a decade of dialogue with guitarists worldwide as the editor of *Acoustic Guitar* magazine and moderator of its online forum for beginners, I heard beginners ask the same types of questions again and again. The most common and perplexing ones are collected and answered here, and all those mystifying bits of guitarese you'll hear are defined along the way (look in the Index of Guitar Lingo to find where a particular word or phrase is fully explained and illustrated). Whether you are at home trying to figure out what to practice or how to change strings, or in a music store shopping for a guitar or a capo, you'll find reliable and understandable advice in these pages.

Throughout the book you will hear pearls of wisdom from a wide range of teachers and instrument experts. I can't tell you how many times I have thought, "I wish I had known *that* when I was learning to play!" during the course of putting together this book. I hope *Teach Yourself Guitar Basics* clears up nagging questions, steers you away from some dead ends, and most of all, inspires you to fill your home with your own music—there's nothing better.

Happy playing,
Jeffrey Pepper Rodgers

 **Introduction and Tune-Up**

YOUR FIRST LESSONS

Chords 101

Pete Madsen

So you have decided to play guitar, eh? An excellent choice! Whether your tastes run from classical to rock, jazz, or folk, the guitar can provide the inspiration to create wonderful music. In this lesson, we will focus on first-position chords, which are made by placing your fingers in various positions on the first three frets. These chords provide a big, open sound and are used constantly by both novice and experienced players. Once you learn just three of them, you'll be able to play a song. With double that number under your belt (we'll actually learn nine chords in this lesson), most of the world's pop, alternative, rock, and folk tunes will be at your beck and call.

A Note on Notation

To begin with, let's get some names and numbers straight. The fingers on your left (fretting) hand will be referred to as index (first), middle (second), ring (third), and pinky (fourth). Now for the guitar strings: the E (sixth) string is the lowest- (or deepest-) sounding string. It's also the thickest string and the one closest to your face as you hold the guitar in your lap. The strings below that (heading toward the floor and getting progressively thinner) are the A (fifth) string, D (fourth), G (third), B (second), and E (first). The letter refers to the note sounded by the open string (played with no left-hand fingers touching the string), while the numbers are an easy tool for talking about which string to use. Last but not least, consider the frets: those thin, raised metal bars embedded in your fretboard. They are numbered from the nut to the bridge, or more simply, from left to right as you look down at your guitar. Got all that? OK, now we can move on to the chords.

Your First Chord—G

The G chord has a rich, full sound, thanks to its combination of fretted strings (played with the left-hand fingers pressing on the fretboard) and open strings (played with no left-hand fingers touching them). Start by putting your index finger on the fifth

string at the second fret. (At the fret actually means just behind the fret—to the left of it as you look down.) For the best tone, place your finger as close to the back of the fret as possible. Next, place your middle finger on the low E (sixth) string at the third fret. Now you have a choice to make; you can use either your ring finger or your pinky on the high E (sixth) string at the third fret. Try both and see which one is most comfortable.

Now it's time to strum that puppy! Using a pick or the back of your index finger, start a strum with a downstroke: start at the low E (sixth) string and work your way down through the high E (first) string. How does it sound? Great? Not so great? If it sounds great, then wonderful! You have now strummed your first chord.

Strumming with a pick? Here's how to hold it.

Troubleshooting

If your strings are out of tune, your chords won't sound good—so first be sure you're tuned up properly. See the Getting in Tune and Getting Started section of the FAQ for a complete rundown on tuning.

If your guitar is in tune but the chord sounds jangly and odd, first check that you have the right fingers on the right strings (use that chord diagram!). If it sounds good except for a few muted or buzzing sounds, here are a few things to try.

First, check your finger pressure. Make sure you are applying enough pressure to the strings to make them ring clearly—but not too much pressure, because you don't want to start any repetitive stress injuries. And don't forget to trim your nails—long nails can make even pressure and good hand position difficult.

If you're still having trouble, take a look at your hand position: your left thumb should be situated behind the neck of the guitar, preferably at the fattest part of the neck. If your thumb is creeping toward the top of the neck, try moving it down and notice what happens to your fingers. They should roll out, away from the neck. This will help your fingers rest only on the strings they are fretting—when a finger touches another string even lightly, it will deaden the sound of that string. Notice your wrist, as well. If you imagine a string tied to it, pulling it gently toward the floor, it should also help your hand to rotate out.

Last but not least, note your guitar position. Many beginners are tempted to hold the guitar slanted on their laps so they can see their left-hand fingers, but this makes good hand position difficult. Try to hold the guitar perpendicular to your legs (if you're sitting down). You may have to crane your neck a little to see your fingers, but you'll find it much easier to make the chords ring.

Once you've made all these adjustments, try playing through the chord one string at a time to ferret out any trouble spots, and you should be good to go. If your fingers feel tender after all this effort, never fear—in just a few weeks you'll build up some helpful calluses, the mark of a veteran guitar player.

Strum It

Let's put this all together with **Example 1**. Strum through the G chord four times in each measure (delineated by the thin vertical lines). Each diagonal slash represents a beat, and you strum once per beat, making a grand total of 16 strums. Start at the low E (sixth) string and strum down through the high E (first) string. It's a good idea to tap your foot once for each strum, counting "one two three four, one two three four" (this will come in handy later). Try to keep a steady, even rhythm.

C and D Chords

Two chords that go well with a G chord are the C and D chords. To make a C chord, place your index finger on the second string at the first fret, your middle finger on the fourth string at the second fret, and your ring finger on the fifth string at the third fret. Make sure that your thumb is behind the neck! Before you strum, note the *X* on the top left corner of the C chord diagram. That means you don't play the sixth string. Instead, you'll start the downstroke on the A (fifth) string. Try playing four measures of the C chord, as in **Example 2**.

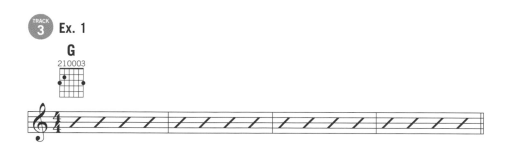

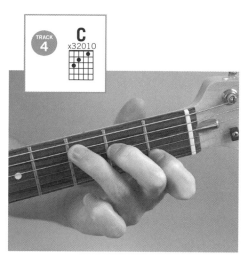

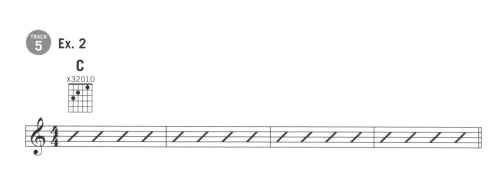

To make a D chord, place your index finger on the third string at the second fret, your middle finger on the first string at the second fret, and your ring finger on the second string at the third fret. Notice in the chord diagram that the sixth and fifth strings are off-limits this time, so start your strum on the open D (fourth) string. Now, strum through four measures of the D chord (**Example 3**).

Switching Chords

Congratulations! You now have three chords to work with: G, C, and D. This combination is the golden key to all kinds of pop tunes, including classics like "La Bamba" and "Twist and Shout." So, you're ready to rock! But, if you're a new guitar player, there's a hurdle to get through first: learning to switch chords smoothly. Take a minute right now and try it. Switch between G and C, then G and D, and then C and D. It will be slow and awkward at first, but remember: you are developing new muscle memories. Like any new physical skill, this takes a little time—days, weeks, or months depending on how much you practice—before it becomes automatic. Until then, you'll want to take the following exercises slowly. But keep at it!

> Once you learn just three chords, you'll be able to play a song.

Try **Example 4**, which switches between all three chords in a steady, even rhythm. You'll be playing all downstrokes and tapping your foot with each strum. Notice that the slashes have been replaced in the example by quarter notes. The notation is different but the rhythm is the same as with the slashes. Play G four

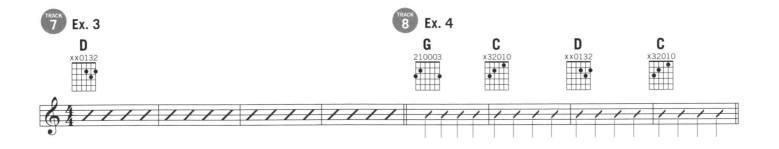

times, then C four times, then D four times, and back to C (do you hear the chorus to "La Bamba" yet?). Start slowly! You'll probably find yourself pausing for a few seconds or more to change chords. That's OK at the beginning, but as soon as your changes get smoother, you should practice changing chords in time, even if it means playing at a snail's pace. (Using a metronome set at a slow tempo can help you keep a regular beat.)

Strum Rhythms

Now let's try a different kind of strum rhythm. **Example 5** shows a new rhythm indicated with quarter notes and eighth notes. Put down your pick and try tapping out this rhythm on the back of your guitar. As your foot taps "one two three four, one two three four" on the floor, add a tap after beats two and four with your hand. These in-between beats are eighth notes (two of which equal a quarter note) and are sometimes referred to as the *and* of the beat. You can count this rhythm as "one two-and three four-and."

Let's transfer that rhythm to strumming a G chord, as shown in **Example 6**. First, get your left-hand fingers into position. Next, start tapping your foot (slowly!). Now, add the strums. Each time your foot lands on the floor, play a downstroke. When your foot lifts up from the floor after the second and fourth beats, add an upstroke: that means you sweep your pick quickly back across the strings as your right hand returns to its starting point. Once that's somewhat comfortable, move on to **Example 7**, which uses the same strum rhythm while changing chords using the "La Bamba" chord progression.

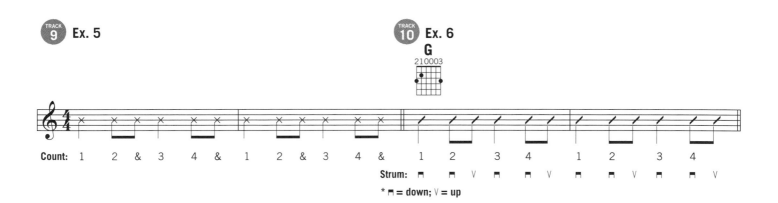

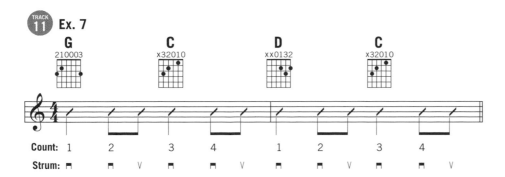

E and A Chords

Let's learn one more chord so we can play a progression similar to Outkast's "Hey Ya!" The E chord is a guitar player's best friend—learn it and love it! Put your index finger on the G string at the first fret, your middle finger on the A string at the second fret, and your ring finger on the D string at the second fret. As with the G chord, you get to strum all the strings here.

Example 8 shows the "Hey Ya!" progression with a new strumming pattern—a simplification of the one we just learned. Here, the pattern is: down down-up down down. The only difference is you don't play the upstroke after the fourth beat.

To make an A chord, you can use either your index, middle, and ring fingers or your middle, ring, and pinky fingers. All those fingers will be crammed in at the sec-

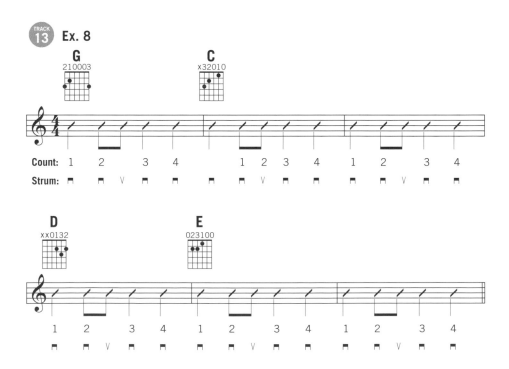

ond fret on the fourth, third, and second strings respectively. You can also use your index, middle, and ring fingers in another configuration. Try swapping your index and middle fingers, so your index finger is on the third string and your middle is on the fourth string (this may seem awkward, but it will actually make changing to the D and E chords easier). Strum every string except the sixth string. Now try **Example 9**, which is similar to the Romantics' huge '80s hit "That's What I Like About You."

In the same way that G, C, and D chords work well together, the E, A, and D chords also work well together. For example, you can use them to play that same "La Bamba"–style progression at a different pitch. (Try playing A, D, E, D instead of G, C, D, C and you'll see what I mean.) I won't go into great detail here about why certain chords work well together, but the upshot is that if you're ready to sing along with your guitar, you may find one set of chords better suited to your vocal range than the other.

Minor Chords

The next example uses two minor chords; luckily, these are easy transitions from the major chords you already know. To make an E-minor chord (Em), start by playing an E chord. Then remove your ring finger from the third string. Voilà—Em!

To play A minor (Am), start by making the A-major chord with your middle, ring, and pinky fingers (remember the fingering options for A?). To go from A to Am, simply remove your pinky from the second string and place your index finger on the second string at the first fret.

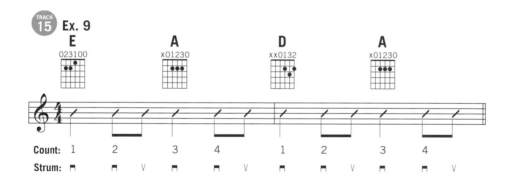

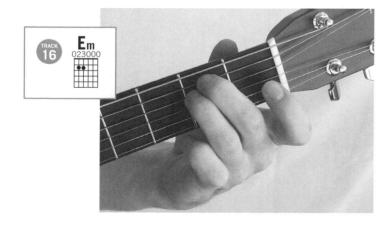

Try these new chords out in **Example 10**, which is a chord progression from the Yardbirds' song "For Your Love." Play just one strum per measure.

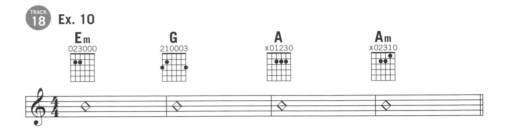

The last example is a cool progression that involves just two new chords. To make a D-minor chord, place your index finger on the high E at the first fret, your middle finger on the G string at the second fret, and your ring finger on the B string at the third fret. Now strum all the strings except the two lowest.

The transition from an A chord to an A7 is pretty simple. If you are using your index, middle, and ring fingers to make an A, simply remove your middle finger, leaving the G string open, and strum all the strings except the low E string. You can also play A7 with your middle finger on the fourth string and your ring finger on the second string, as shown in the photo. The **Example 11** chord pattern is similar to the song "I Heard It Through the Grapevine."

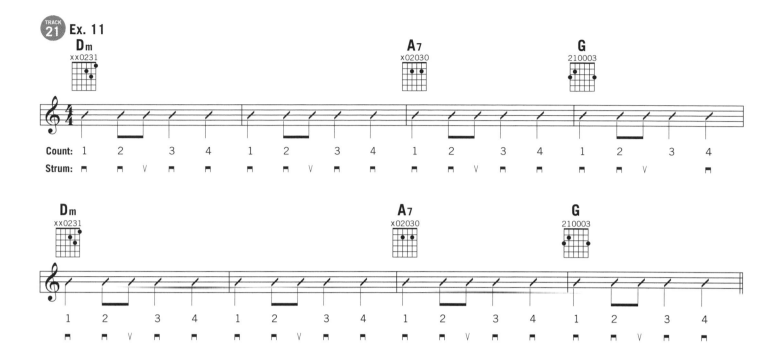

Now that you have nine chords under your belt, you have the tools to play thousands of songs. Try using the chords in different combinations. See which chords work well together and which don't. Try figuring out songs on your own—using your new chords, your ear, and a CD or MP3 player, you can probably guess what some of the chords are in many popular songs. You might also try picking the notes of the chords one at a time instead of strumming. Finally, try making something up; you are only limited by your imagination.

More Chords

Want to get some more chords under your fingers? See the "Essential Chord Library" in the back of the book.

Intro to Power Chords

Josh Workman

If you came to love the guitar through metal, punk rock, grunge, or anything else derived from rock 'n' roll, then power chords are in your blood, whether you know it or not. Unlike standard guitar chords, **power chords** are simplified chord shapes played on two or three strings and can be moved all over the neck. If you're a fan of big, crunchy guitar tone à la AC/DC or Metallica, then you need to start playing power chords.

Open-Position Power Chords

To get an idea of where the power of power chords comes from, strum the first E chord below. That E chord is a major chord (made up of the notes E, G♯, and B), and the G♯ that your index finger is fretting is what makes it major. Lift your index finger and strum the E-minor chord (notated Em). You'll notice it sounds a little sad—that's because of the open G note. Now, play the E power chord (E5). Hear how open it sounds? That's because it has only the E and B notes. Power chords are neither minor nor major so you can use the E5 in place of either E or Em in songs. (For more on the theory behind chords, see "Power-Chord Theory," on page 22.)

Now you can hear the sound of rock starting to unfold under your fingers, especially on a steel-stringed acoustic or an electric guitar with distortion turned on. Take A (major) and Am through the same paces as E, below. The only difference is that the root note (the lowest note of the power chord) is on the fifth string instead of the sixth string. Since E5 and A5 use open (unfretted) strings, they're called open-position chords.

Practice narrowing and widening the arc or sweep of your pick so you strum just the three strings you need for the chord. Use your ear to determine how many strings you hit and increase the arc to hit more and decrease to hit less. You can also lightly mute any unwanted strings by letting your fretting-hand fingers barely touch the adjacent strings.

Generate Any Power Chord

With the movable power chord shape and this diagram, you can play any power chord you need. Just find the root note (the note the chord is named after) on the fifth or sixth string, then play the movable shape with your index finger on the root.

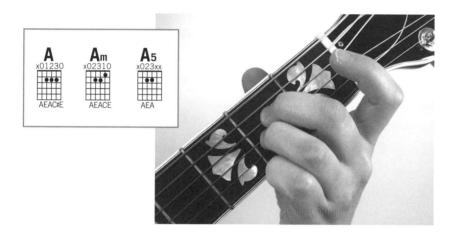

Movable Power Chords

To show you how to form the basic movable power-chord shape, fret the E5 using your ring and pinky fingers. Slide your fingers up a fret, place your index finger on the first fret of the sixth string (the F note), and you've got an F5. In the movable shape, your index finger frets the root note.

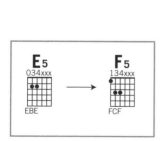

Now try the same thing with an A5. Start by fretting the A5 with your ring and pinky fingers. Slide up two frets, add in your index finger on the second fret of the fifth string (a B note), and you've got a B5. In this shape, the root is on the fifth string.

Use "Generate Any Power Chord" on page 17 to figure out other chords.

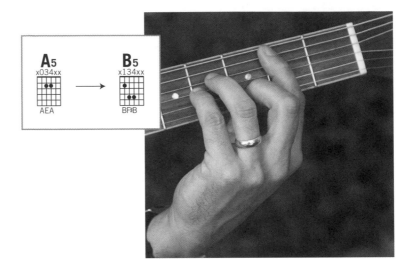

Rev Up Your Riffs

Our first riff, **Example 1**, is similar to the song "My Best Friend's Girl" by the Cars. You will notice that all the power chords here are movable shapes, so this should be pretty easy. To give your power chords a heavy, chunky sound, use all downstrokes to strum this and all the riffs in this lesson. Count out loud and strum on the italicized beats. In measure one your strums will go: *one-and two-and* three-*and four-and*. In measure two, strum the whole thing: *one-and two-and three-and four-and*. To sound more like the original recording, try muting the strings throughout by lightly resting the palm of your picking hand on the strings down near the bridge.

Practice Plan

When you first play through the riffs, count out loud and take them slow (50–60 bpm). Once you get a handle on the rhythms, work through them for about 10–15 minutes a day, increasing your tempo gradually in increments of four bpm up to the goal tempo.

Beginner tip: Play only the lowest two notes of the chords until you feel comfortable switching between chords at about 70–80 bpm.

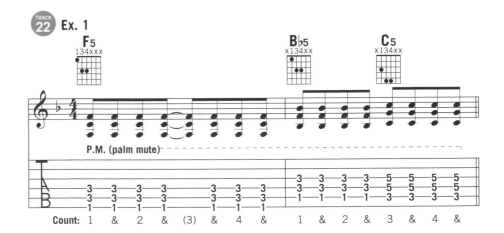

Our next riff, **Example 2**, is similar to the song "I Love Rock 'n' Roll," popularized by Joan Jett and the Blackhearts. If you find it difficult to make the change between A5 and B5, slow down and try to be aware of your fingers as they move back and forth. Observe how each finger moves to the next position. Try to keep your fingers from flying up off the strings and keep them hovering just above the strings like piano hammers. Count out loud and strum on the italicized beats: *one*-and two-and *three*-and four-and. You can use the palm of your picking hand to mute the strings on beats 2 and 4.

Practice this two-measure phrase slowly with a metronome to get used to changing chords. Gradually increase the tempo to about 90 beats per minute and you'll be in business.

Example 3 is derived from Deep Purple's "Smoke on the Water," which features one of the most distinctive power-chord riffs in rock history. This variation introduces some syncopation (off-beat rhythms) to the mix, especially in measure 2. If you're familiar with the actual song, you'll probably be able to play the rhythm by ear. In measure 1, strum the chords on beats one, two, and three, then start playing on the *ands*, returning to the downbeat on beat three of the

Just Add Distortion

If you have an electric guitar and want crunchy sustain, you need to experiment with **distortion**—either through an amp with built-in distortion or an effects pedal.

Does your amp have a master volume knob? Yes? Then you're in luck! All you have to do is turn the master down and start raising the preamp volume (also called drive or gain) until you hear the crunch start to kick in. If your amp has a midrange control, decrease the mids and raise the bass for a tighter, tougher metal sound or increase the mids a little and go easy on the preamp volume for a bluesy tone. For those of you without a master volume, you can either turn the amp way up to overdrive the speaker or buy a distortion or overdrive pedal for as little as $20.

If you use a distortion pedal, you'll apply the same approaches as with the amp, turning the preamp (often marked "distortion" on pedals) up, while turning the output volume down.

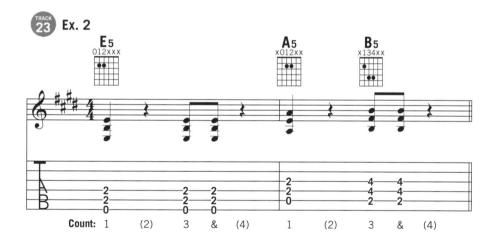

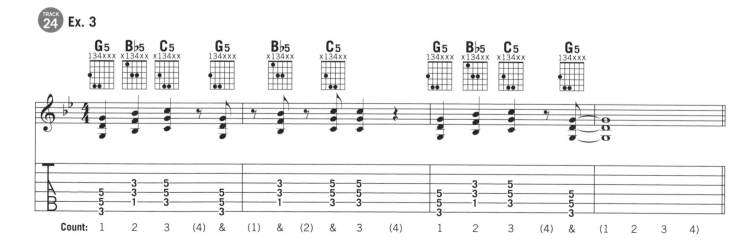

second measure. Measure 3 is the same as measure 1, but the G5 ties over to a whole note (a note held for four beats) in measure 4. Gradually work your way up to about 108 bpm to sound like the recorded version.

Example 4 uses movable power chords and is similar to "You Really Got Me" by the Kinks and later covered by Van Halen. The first chord (F5) is a pickup (a note or chord that's played before the first measure starts) and is played on the *and* of beat four, followed by G5 for one-and, then slide down to the F5 on two and up to the G5

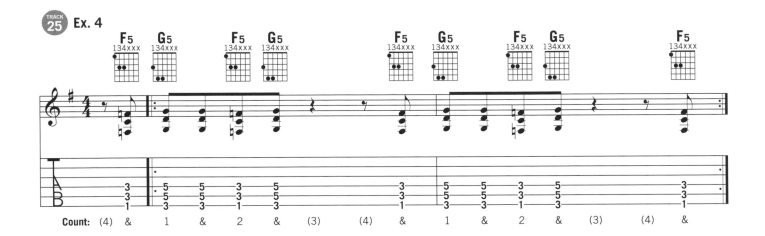

Power-Chord Theory

Most songs are made up of a series of chords that work together to help support a melody. The melody often comes from a scale (a series of single notes that progress stepwise up or down in a particular order), the most recognizable of which is the seven-note major scale (do, re, mi, etc.).

If you build a power chord on each of the seven notes in the E-major scale, you'll get the E-major scale in power chords. Examples 1 and 2 are both called I–IV–V (pronounced "one four five") chord progressions. This means that E5, A5, and B5 are built on the first, fourth, and fifth notes (also called degrees or scale tones) of the E-major scale, just as F5, B♭5, and C5 are built on scale tones 1, 4, and 5 of an F-major scale.

To learn more about scales and chord theory, see "Music Theory Made Easy" on page 34.

E-Major Scale in Power Chords

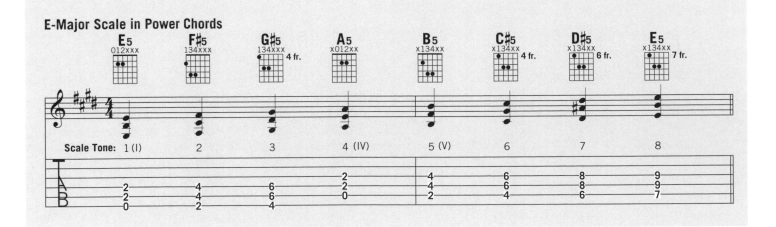

for the *and*. Rest on beat three and the first half of beat four, then repeat. To play it like the Kinks or Van Halen, aim for a goal tempo of about 136 bpm.

Make Your Own High-Voltage Riffs

Now that you've harnessed the power of these chords, try using them instead of major or minor chords in simple songs that you already know. You can also use them to hear the general outline of a song that you might be writing or hear on the radio, then go back and see whether it makes sense to plug major or minor chords into certain places (based on the sound of the melody) or just leave a fat power chord there. Let your ears be your guide, and don't be afraid to unleash the power of these chords.

Power-Chord Songs

Power chords aren't just for metal anymore. Check out how they're used in these songs from all over the rock realm.

"DOA" by Foo Fighters

"Fortunate Son" by Creedence Clearwater Revival

"Layla" by Derek and the Dominos

"Seven Nation Army" by the White Stripes

"Smells Like Teen Spirit" by Nirvana

"TNT" by AC/DC

Ten Great 4/4 Rhythm Patterns

Adam Perlmutter

In the rush to play cool riffs and lead lines, beginning guitarists often overlook one of the guitar's most important functions—to provide a solid rhythmic background. By learning a handful of basic rhythm patterns and variations, you can easily create the solid foundation that's necessary for playing in a variety of styles. In the process, your musicianship will benefit immensely.

Common time, or 4/4 time, is the time signature that appears most often in Western music, from classical to jazz to rock. In this lesson, we'll focus on 4/4 time with a few examples of popular rhythmic patterns you can use immediately in your playing.

An Introduction to 4/4 Time

Before we get started, it's important to explore the basics of 4/4 time. The time signature is indicated with a pair of stacked 4s (or sometimes, a ℂ symbol) at the beginning of the first measure of a piece of music, as seen in **Example 1a**. The top 4 indicates that each measure has four beats, and the bottom 4 indicates that each beat of the measure is worth one quarter note (think one quarter = 1/4). The 4/4 measures in **Example 1b** illustrate various note and rest durations in this time signature: whole notes occupy all four beats of a given measure, half notes last for two beats, and quarter notes each last for one. Beats can also be divided into two eighth notes, and a dot after a note or a rest means it should be held for 1½ times its normal value. So, a dotted quarter note lasts for 1½ beats, the same length as a quarter note plus an eighth note.

Ex. 1a

The rhythmic patterns in this lesson will mostly involve eighth and quarter notes. When you're playing the examples throughout, it's a good idea to count along as indicated between the staves. While only the accented syllables are sounded on the guitar, recite all the syllables to help maintain a consistent sense of rhythm.

TRACK 26 **Ex. 1b**

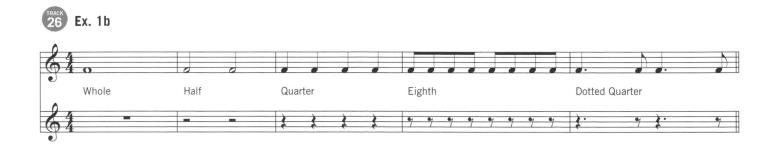

Whole   Half   Quarter   Eighth   Dotted Quarter

Basic Eighth-Note Patterns

The next few examples depict a few common eighth-note strums (again, two per beat) that are easy but satisfying to play. To play the straight eighth-note pattern in **Example 2**, grip the C chord throughout and strum in a continuous and even down-and-up motion: down on the beat and up on the *ands*.

In **Example 3**, the eighth-note strum is made a little more interesting by the addition of a quarter note on beat one, similar to the pattern used in Bob Seger's "Night Moves." Don't let the quarter note throw off your rhythm in this pattern. Here's a tip: keep your picking hand moving in a continuous up-down motion, but on the upstroke and of beat one, lift your picking hand so that it passes over the strings.

The strum pattern in **Example 4** is similar to the one Bob Dylan plays in "Mr. Tambourine Man." Note that we're using a four-finger version of a G chord that includes a D note at the third fret on the second string. This pattern includes some syncopation—accenting of a weak beat—in the middle of each bar. To play it, use alternating eighth-note strums, but pass over the strings on the *ands* of beats one and two, as well as on beat three. The curved lines between beats two and three are ties, which instruct you to hold the tied notes for the total duration of the notes they connect. This example also demonstrates a neat chord-switching trick: at the end of the first bar, on the *and* of beat four, strumming open strings gives your hands a little time to move from the D chord to the G.

Inspired by Jimi Hendrix's version of Dylan's "All Along the Watchtower," **Example 5** is eighth note–based. To achieve the desired rhythmic effect, use the same continuous strumming as in the previous examples, and avoid striking the strings on the *and* of beat two as well as three. Also, after you play the Am chord

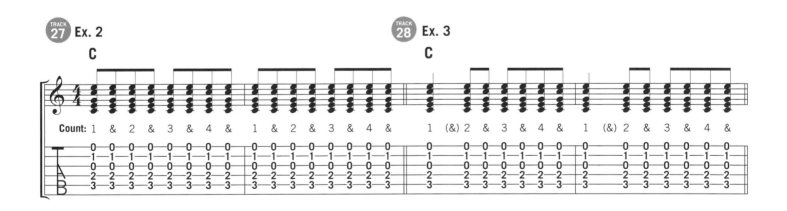

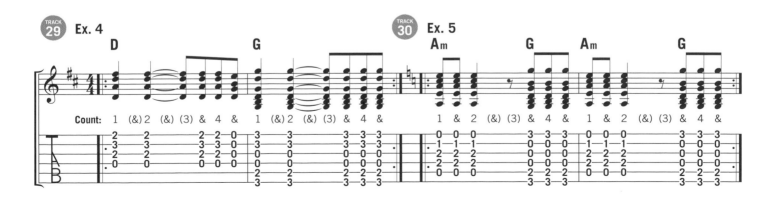

on beat two, release your fretting-hand grip slightly to stop the chord from sounding (often in music, the notes you don't play are as significant as the ones you do).

Styles and Players

Sometimes a single 4/4 pattern neatly sums up the entire rhythmic approach of a genre or performer. **Example 6**, for instance, demonstrates a **boom-chuck** pattern, the most common rhythm in bluegrass, country, and beyond. Put simply, the "boom" is the single bass note (falling on beats one and three) and the "chuck" is the higher chord (beats two and four). Play this with solid downstrokes for a driving feel. As a variation you can toss in an upstroke strum on the *ands* of beats two and four.

The rock and blues guitarist Bo Diddley used one particular rhythm to such a successful degree that it came to be known as the "Bo Diddley beat." This rhythm has a Latin-inspired syncopation (also referred to as a clave) and is heard in everything from "Desire" by U2 to "Mr. Brownstone" by Guns N' Roses. While Bo Diddley played the rhythm on his trademark rectangular electric guitar, it sounds just as good on acoustic, as you can hear in **Example 7**. Note that unlike the previous examples, this rhythm pattern repeats every two measures, instead of every measure.

Inspired by boogie-woogie piano, the **shuffle** is the heart of the blues and most blues-inspired music. While the pattern is written as straight eighth notes, it is actually played as a triplet for a **swing feel**. Each beat is divided into three equal parts, with the first eighth note occupying the first two parts and the following eighth note occupying the third. Think long-short, long-short, etc. To play a basic shuffle, as

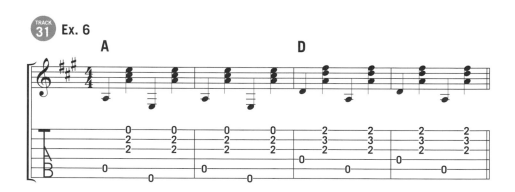

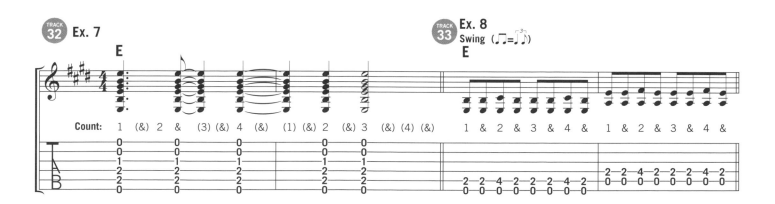

shown in the two-note chords of **Example 8**, use all downstrokes and emphasize each downbeat (one, two, three, and four). You can also mute the strings with the heel of your picking hand.

In an uptempo blues number, a guitarist might play a less involved but snappy rhythm that is essentially two half notes, with the second half note in each bar being anticipated by half a beat (falling on the *and* of two), as shown in **Example 9**. You might try placing a little emphasis on the second chord in each bar.

The basic pattern for swing rhythm guitar is often known as Freddie Green style, named for the guitarist who played with Count Basie for many years. In Green's simple but effective approach, music is stripped to its essence—most often, just downstrummed quarter notes and a couple of notes (sometimes even one!) that imply fuller chords. In **Example 10**, G7 and C7 are played with just thirds and sevenths (F and B, for the G7; E and B♭ for the C7). For an added percussive effect, try muting the higher strings with the underside of your fretting hand's index finger.

> By learning a handful of basic rhythm patterns and variations, you can easily create the solid foundation that's necessary for playing in a variety of styles.

So far we've focused mostly on downbeats, but a reggae-inspired riddim like **Example 11** will get you started feeling those upbeats (the *ands*). Here we're using an F chord on the top four strings. This pattern relies heavily on silence—as indicated by the eighth-note rests—so be sure to mute each chord right after you play it by releasing your fretting hand's grip. This example is perhaps the most

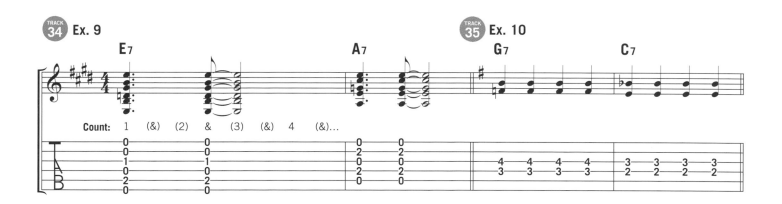

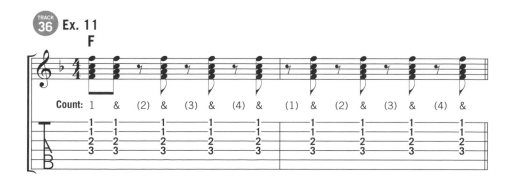

difficult to execute, so take things slowly and be sure to carefully count along as you play it.

Play a 12-Bar Blues

As this lesson has been all about the diversity of 4/4 patterns, it's only fitting to wrap things up by plugging the materials into one of the most durable of all musical forms—the 12-bar blues. In case you're unfamiliar with that structure, two full choruses are mapped out for you in "**12-Bar Rhythm Study**" in the key of E major, using E7, A7, and B7 chords. Try to play through the 12-bar pattern using each of the rhythm examples shown in this lesson.

   The first 12 bars are shown with the rhythm example from Example 4, but any of the examples in this lesson will work fine. The chord charts shown above each measure will work fine for most examples, although the blues shuffle (Example 8) and the Freddie Green chord exercise (Example 10) require some different shapes that are shown near the bottom of the page. The rhythm figures in Examples 7 and 11 are both two measures long. They don't work as well over the chords that only last for one measure before the next change (like the E7 in measure 1, which lasts for just one bar before moving to A7), so to play these rhythms, consider doubling the number of measures given to each chord, and then play the full two-measure rhythm figure once for each bar shown in the music.

Let's wrap things up by plugging the materials into one of the most durable of all musical forms— the 12-bar blues.

12-Bar Rhythm Study

Music by Adam Perlmutter

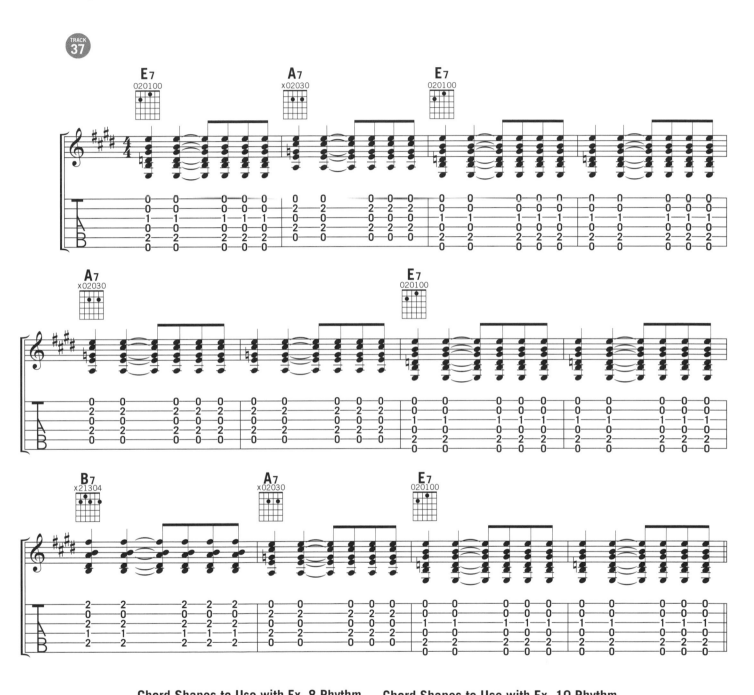

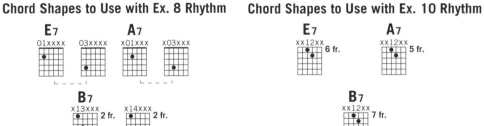

The ABCs of Fingerpicking

David Hodge

t's very easy for beginners to be a bit intimidated by fingerstyle guitar playing. After all, who can listen to Leo Kottke—or Lindsey Buckingham, or any other fingerstyle wiz—and not wonder how on earth one might ever be able to play such beautiful and intricate music? The good news is that, like most things about the guitar, getting started on fingerpicking is actually pretty simple. In fact, if you look at fingerstyle as a slightly more elaborate way of strumming chords—playing the chords one string at a time instead of all at once, as in an **arpeggio**—it can be as easy as ABC.

Arpeggio

Thinking about fingerpicking as simply a different way to strum chords also provides you with a safety net of sorts: As long as you hold a chord's shape, you can't make a bad-sounding mistake in picking. If you hit a string other than the one you intended, it's very likely that no one else is going to know.

To try this out, start with some basic, open-position arpeggios. The idea here is just to get your fingers working at the task. Remember, they're not used to doing this, so have patience. Begin **Example 1** by using your thumb to play the three ascending notes of each set and your fingers to play the descending ones.

Which fingers? While there are many different styles of fingerpicking, as a beginner it's a good idea to try to get them all (except your pinky) involved. Typically, you want to think of your fingers as being "assigned" to a particular string. The thumb gets the bass notes, so it is in charge of any notes on the lower three strings. Your ring finger plays any notes on the first string, your middle finger takes the notes of the second string, and your index finger is responsible for the third string.

But the third string can also be claimed by the thumb. Try **Example 2** both ways: First, use your thumb on the third note of the arpeggio and your index finger

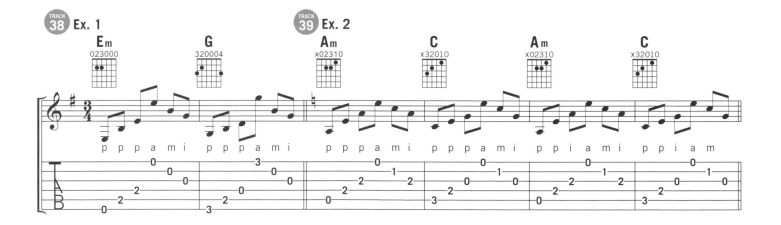

on the sixth note (as shown in the first two measures); then, play the notes of the third string exclusively with the index finger (in the last two measures). It's good to be comfortable with both techniques.

Bring On the Bass

Once your fingers are limber and ready to take on more of a challenge, you can get to work on some basic "Travis picking." Named after Merle Travis, who popularized this style of playing in the middle of the last century, the technique involves adding a steady bass line, played with the thumb, alternating with notes played by the fingers.

Let's begin with just the bass for the open-position G chord, shown in **Example 3**. Your thumb is going to alternate between the low G note (third fret of the sixth string) and the D note of the open fourth string, each note getting one beat. You may find it helps to count the beats aloud as you play. One of the unforeseen benefits of fingerstyle playing is that you often develop a great sense of rhythm. Here your thumb is acting as your metronome, steadily keeping the beat as it plays.

Now comes the fun part. We're going to play a note with a finger in between each note that the thumb plays. Pick any string, or any finger—as long as you've got your chord formed on the fingerboard, it's going to sound fine. **Example 4** demonstrates an easy pattern for you to start with.

Start out slowly and deliberately, and don't be afraid to count it out as you play. You'll probably be surprised at how quickly your fingers take to the pattern, almost as if they were on automatic pilot. It won't be long before you can do it with your eyes closed.

Now try a different pattern, such as the one in **Example 5**. Also be sure to use different chords (bearing in mind that the bass note you'll want to start out on may be on a different string).

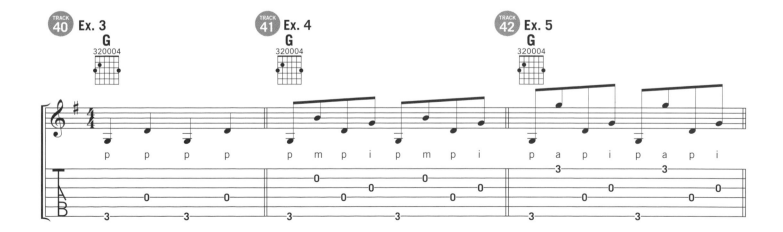

You'll probably be surprised at how quickly your fingers take to the pattern.

Example 6 applies these two basic patterns to different chords. Notice that in the last measure of this example (the D chord), you are using your thumb to play the third string.

Change Gears

Since songs rarely use only one chord, you'll want to be able to change chords while playing a pattern. Begin by switching between chords that use the same string for the root note—for example, G and Em, or C and Am (the latter is shown in **Example 7**). Then test yourself by switching between chords that use different strings for their roots, as in the G-to-Am-to-D7 progression of **Example 8**.

And don't forget that you can add all sorts of touches, such as walking bass lines, to your playing. **Example 9** shows one way of spicing up the switches you made in Example 8.

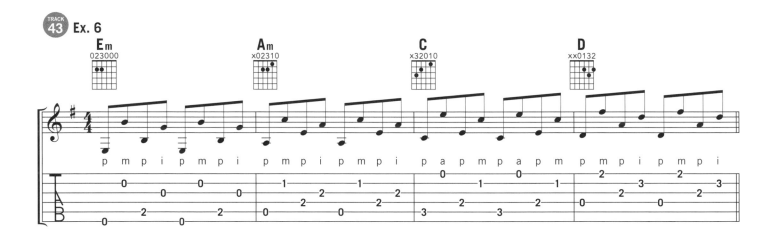

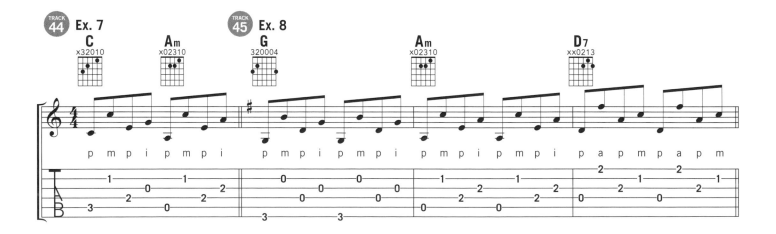

Get Up to Speed

Once your fingers can play patterns easily, the task becomes keeping them at a steady tempo and not racing ahead of the beat. Speed up a familiar slow tempo to build your skill here. **Example 10**, despite its appearance, is the same pattern as the one used in Example 4, only here your thumb is counting off eighth notes instead of quarter notes.

Let's put this idea, along with the other patterns and techniques we've used thus far, to good use by playing a simple arrangement of "**Greenland Whale Fisheries**," an old sea chantey from long ago that is still played today by artists as diverse as the Pogues and Peter, Paul, and Mary.

Be patient with your fingers, and you will soon find yourself trying out new picking patterns on a regular basis. You'll also begin to hear patterns on recorded music and, before you know it, you'll be taking a stab at figuring them out yourself. Welcome to the wonderful world of fingerpicking guitar!

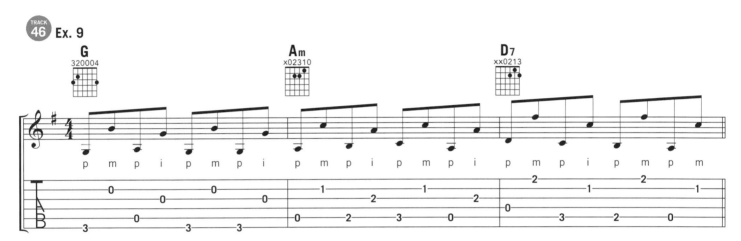

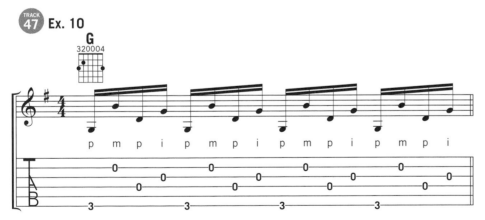

Greenland Whale Fisheries

Traditional, arranged by David Hodge

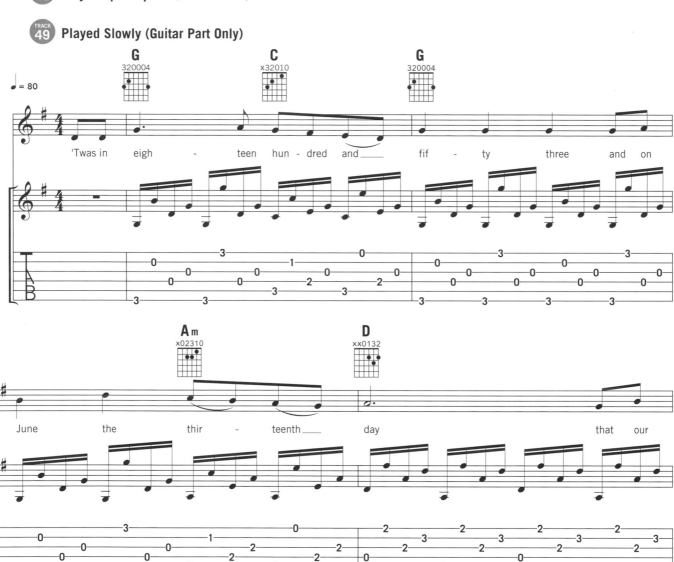

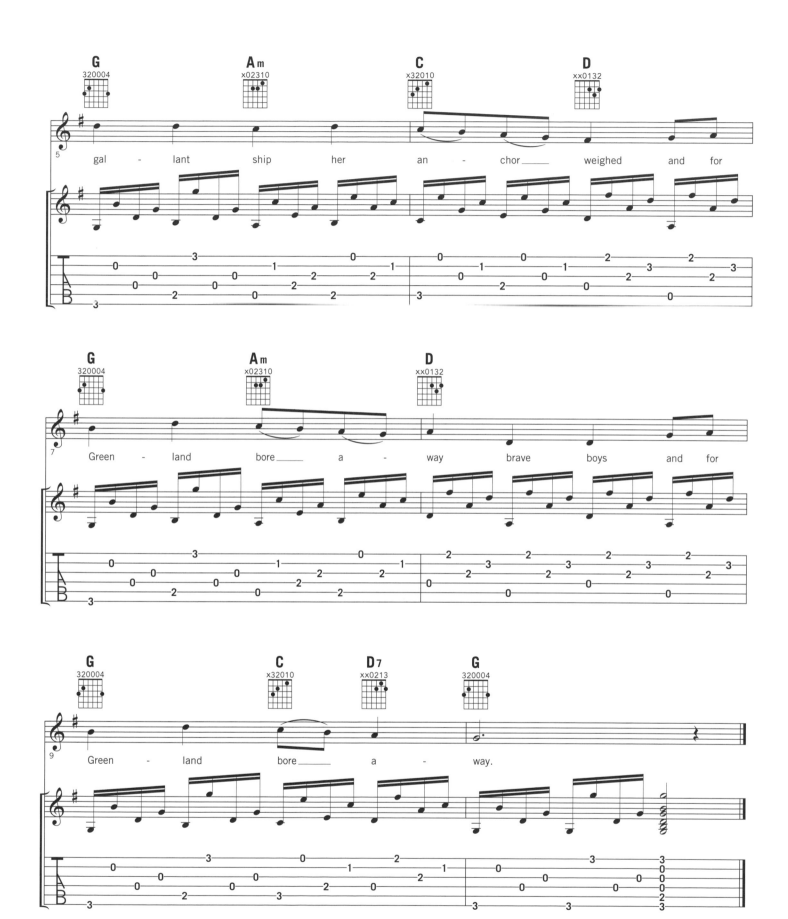

Music Theory Made Easy

Adam Levy

You don't need the skills of a NASCAR driver to drive to the store for a carton of eggs. Neither do you need a Ph.D. in music theory to play guitar. But just as everyday drivers need to know rules of the road before getting behind the wheel, there are a few basics of music theory that every player can benefit from learning. Understanding scale and chord fundamentals helps you communicate clearly with other musicians and make sense of melodies and chord progressions.

12-Point Inspection: Scale Basics

Let's start off by examining one of the most common scales, C major (**Example 1**).

As you can see, this scale has seven notes, plus the second C that's one octave above our starting point. The distance from any note to the same letter note eight tones above or below is an **octave**. If you get to the top of the scale and want to keep going higher, simply repeat the letter names in sequence: C D E F G A B C D E F, and so on. The same can be done in reverse on the lower end: C B A G F E D C B A G, etc. **Example 2** shows an extended C-major scale that starts and ends on G.

The notes in the C-major scale aren't the only ones in our musical universe. There are five other notes, each of which may be named in two different ways. One way uses the **sharp** sign (♯). C♯, for example, is the note one **half step** (one fret position, for us guitarists) above C. Since C is at the first fret of the second string of your guitar, C♯ is at the second fret. The other way to indicate in-between notes is with a **flat** sign (♭). D♭ is the note one half step below D. Since D is at the third fret of the second string, D♭ is the note at the second fret. Don't be confused by the fact that, although C♯ and D♭ sound the same and are played the same, they have different names. There's logic behind that, which we'll get to in a minute.

TRACK 50 **Ex. 1: C-major Scale**   **TRACK 51** **Ex. 2: Extended C-major Scale**

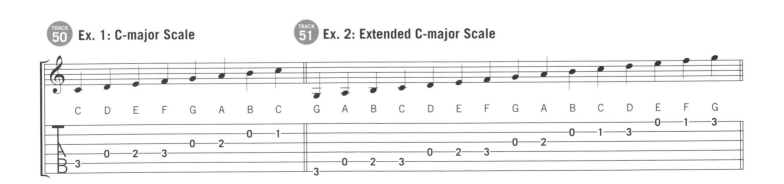

Let's take a look at the mother of all scales—the **chromatic scale**, shown in **Example 3** beginning at the A note. This scale contains all 12 possible notes: A A♯/B♭ B C C♯/D♭ D D♯/E♭ E F F♯/G♭ G G♯/A♭. How do you know there are only 12 notes? Take a look at your guitar. The note at the 12th fret of each string is an octave higher than the open string. If you play the open A string and the note on each of its first 11 frets, you'll get the A chromatic scale.

As we saw earlier, all the sharp notes have flat synonyms (A♯=B♭, C♯=D♭, D♯=E♭, F♯=G♭, G♯=A♭). Some of the natural notes (notes that are neither flat nor sharp) have alter egos as well (E=F♭, F=E♯, B=C♭, C=B♯). Musical subterfuge? No. As we study how major scales are built, you'll see the reason for these aliases.

The **interval** (distance) between any two neighboring notes in the chromatic scale is one half step, which to us guitarists means one fret. A leap of two half steps (A to B, for example—two frets on a guitar) is called a **whole step**. All major scales are built from a starting note, called a root note, using one simple pattern of half and whole steps: root-whole-whole-half-whole-whole-whole-half. Place this pattern anywhere on your guitar's fretboard, and you've instantly created

Is this note C♯ or D♭? It could be either, depending on which scale you're playing.

a major scale based on that first note and ending at the note an octave higher. In **Example 4**, see how that pattern works on our C-major scale.

Notice also that each letter name is used only once. This is true for all major or minor scales. Another truism is that major or minor scales may contain flats or sharps, but never both.

 Ex. 3: A Chromatic Scale

A   A♯   B   C   C♯   D   D♯   E   F   F♯   G   G♯   A

 Ex. 4: Whole and Half Steps in the C-major Scale

whole   whole   half   whole   whole   whole   half

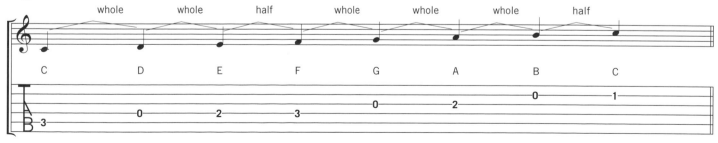

C   D   E   F   G   A   B   C

Let's build an A-major scale following the pattern and rules we just learned. As **Example 5** shows, A to B is a whole step, B to C♯ is a whole step, C♯ to D is a half step, D to E is a whole step, E to F♯ is a whole step, F♯ to G♯ is a whole step, and G♯ to A is a half step. We say C♯ rather than D♭, for example, because of the rules we just learned: we can't have D♭ and D in the same scale, and we can't mix flats and sharps.

Two basic scale types—major and minor—are the basis for most music we hear. Major scales tend to have an upbeat feel, while minors can give music a brooding, melancholy quality. As with major scales, you can build a minor scale anywhere on the fretboard by following a pattern of whole and half steps, in this case: root-whole-half-whole-whole-half-whole-whole. Play through the C-major scale in Example 1 and then the C-minor scale in **Example 6**.

Notice how the C-minor scale evokes a different mood than the C-major scale? Like the C-major scale, the C-minor scale has seven notes (C D E♭ F G A♭ B♭) and can be continued above or below our example.

Keys to the Highway: Chords

On to another of the basic building blocks in music—chords. Built in three-note groups (called triads), chords contain alternating notes from a major or minor scale. Using the C-major scale, we can assemble a chord from the first, third, and fifth notes: C, E, and G.

We can tell if a chord is major or minor by measuring the intervals within it. Using the chromatic scale and our C chord, we can see that from C up to E is four half-steps (called a major third), and from E up to G is three half-steps (a minor third). When a triad's lower third is major and the upper is minor, that chord is **major**, so we've got ourselves a C-major chord (aka C).

Let's build another triad from the C scale, this time starting on D: D, F, A. Measure again—the distance from D up to F is three half-steps (minor third) and from F up to A is four half-steps (major third). When a triad's lower third is minor and the upper third is major, that chord is **minor**. The triad we built from D is a D-minor chord, usually referred to as Dm.

You can also think of chords as the first, third, and fifth notes of a major or minor

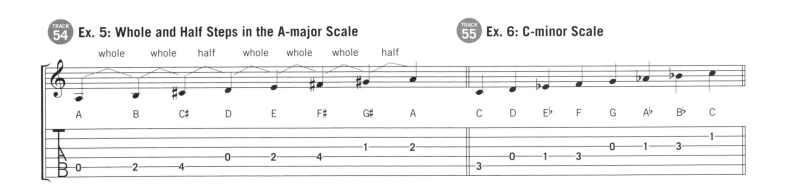

Ex. 5: Whole and Half Steps in the A-major Scale TRACK 54

Ex. 6: C-minor Scale TRACK 55

scale. If you use a major scale, those notes create a major triad. If it's a minor scale, those notes create a minor triad. Using our C-minor scale, we can create a Cm chord.

But let's go back to the C-major scale and build the remaining triads, as shown in **Example 7**. The chord built on B (B, D, F) is unlike the others we've seen so far. Here both intervals (B to D, D to F) are minor, giving us a diminished triad—B diminished (aka Bdim).

Because major scales are always built using the same formula of whole and half steps, the triads built from major scales follow a predictable pattern, regardless of the key. Using the C-major scale, we built C-major, D-minor, E-minor, F-major, G-major, A-minor, and B-diminished triads. If we use the A-major scale, we get the same chord types in the same sequence: A major, B minor, C♯ minor, D major, E major, F♯ minor, and G♯ diminished.

Song Signposts: Roman Numerals

Roman numerals are often used to indicate the chords in any given key. Understanding this system can help you recognize harmonic similarities in different songs and is a crucial step toward transposing songs from one key to another. Uppercase numerals (such as I or IV) are used for major chords, and lowercase (such as ii or iii), for minor and diminished chords. The number refers to where the root note of each chord (the note the chord is named after, also usually the lowest-pitched note) falls within the key you're playing in. The Roman numerals for the chords in the key of C major are shown in **Example 8**.

Players sometimes use these numerals as shorthand to describe chord progressions (the sequence of chords in a song). In the key of C major, the progression C–F–G is written I–IV–V (one of the most common progressions in popular music). In the same key, I–vi–IV–V is C–Am–F–G. That same progression in the key of A major is A–F♯m–D–E. How do we know? In this key, A is the chord built on the first scale degree; F♯m, on the sixth degree; D, on the fourth scale degree; and E, on the fifth scale degree.

Start Your Engines!

We've explored scales and chords in C and A major and introduced you to C minor. To really master the rules of the road, transpose these examples into other keys, starting with the keys of songs you already know, and master their naming conventions. Soon you'll be ready to tackle more advanced scales and chords. In the meantime, you have enough music theory to get you zooming around your fretboard like the six-string equivalent of Dale Earnhardt, Jr.

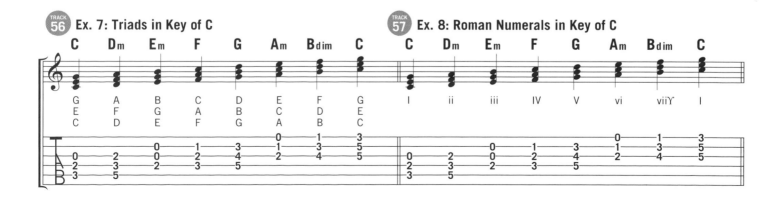

TRACK 56 **Ex. 7: Triads in Key of C**

TRACK 57 **Ex. 8: Roman Numerals in Key of C**

Your First Solo

Jason Garoian

A great guitar solo can seem like it came from another world. While those solos make lead playing seem like terrain only the masters can tread, once you learn the lay of the land and pick up the proper tools—the minor pentatonic scale and a simple chord progression—you, too, will be ready to make the traverse.

Start with an Easy Scale

In this lesson, we're going to use the minor **pentatonic** scale, which is common in all styles of American music from blues to rock to jazz. With fewer notes than an eight-note major or minor scale (pentatonic literally means five notes), the pentatonic is easy to play—you only fret two notes per string—and the notes fit with many chord progressions.

Each finger is assigned a fret to cover, regardless of which string you're playing. The index finger will play notes on the fifth fret, the middle finger plays notes on the sixth fret, the ring finger covers the seventh fret, and the pinky gets the eighth fret. Easy so far, right? Play through the scale a few times (**Example 1**) to help you start off on the right foot.

Use a Basic Chord Progression

When you're taking a solo, you're not completely alone. The chord progression provides a foundation to both launch from and connect with. Some of the most common chord progressions in popular music use the I, IV, and V chords, which start on the first, fourth, and fifth notes, respectively, of an octave scale. So for the key of A, the main chords are A (I), D (IV), and E (V).

Played together, in any order, these three chords don't have much tension or dissonance. Since the minor pentatonic scale doesn't have much tension, either, progressions using the I, IV, and V chords will give us a good solid ground upon which to solo.

When you practice these examples, play them over the chord progressions. You can either record your own (using the chords above the examples) or use the backing tracks on the CD. Since these examples use the same chord progression as the chorus to "Lay Down Sally," you can even play along with Eric Clapton's recording.

TRACK 58 **Ex. 1: A-Minor Pentatonic Scale**

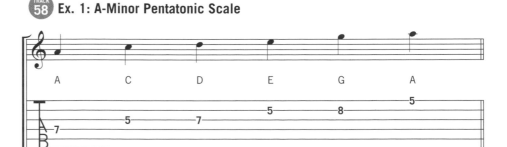

Build an Ascending Line

Let's start putting together your first solo. We'll start with some shorter lines, then add pieces until the solo is complete.

For **Example 2**, begin with your ring finger on the seventh fret of the fifth string. Play with all downstrokes, tapping your foot with each quarter note. Your pick should hit the string as your foot hits the floor. This first exercise is really just the minor pentatonic scale played in order, from A to A, with a half rest at the end. Play this a few times to internalize it, but keep in mind, the scale on its own is just the bare bones. The solo or melody you construct with it is the real living organism.

Example 3 uses the same notes as Example 2 but adds some eighth notes for rhythmic variation. When you play eighth notes, think of your foot and pick as being connected. When your foot goes down (on the numbered beats), your pick goes down; when your foot goes up (on the *ands*), your pick goes up. Play this single-measure line over and over until you're comfortable with it.

Notice that we're starting and ending each lick on the first note of the scale, A, which is also called the root note. This adds a sense of resolution or completion to the licks, and it's one of the things that helps the solo fit smoothly over the chord progression in the same key.

In **Example 4,** we're adding another small phrase at the end of what we've already tackled. That extra bit makes for a two-measure solo. There is a quarter rest for the last beat of this example, which allows you a moment to get your ring finger back in position to play the beginning of the line again. Repeat the line until you can play the whole thing smoothly and seamlessly.

The pentatonic is easy to play—you only fret two notes per string.

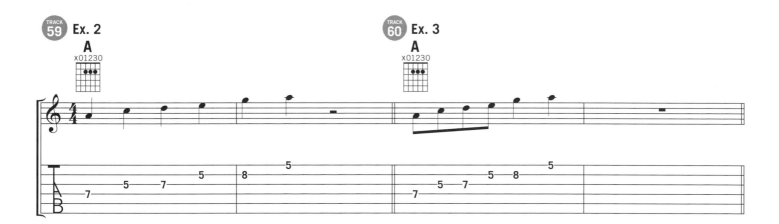

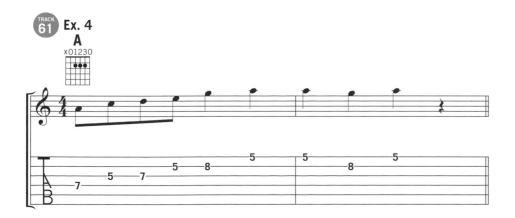

Scales and Repetition

If you learn to play this scale well, before too long you'll develop something called muscle memory. You'll know you're there when your fingers get so used to playing a pattern that you're able to play it without thinking about it too much. Muscle memory is something that you can only get by playing, and the more time you put in, the more you'll internalize the position of the notes. That's where some really great solos are born—from playing by intuition, rather than sitting there trying to think about your fingering. And scales don't have to be boring. Create melodic phrases with them and practicing becomes its own reward.

Example 5 is really just Example 4 with an E (the fifth of the scale) instead of an A as the final note. Ending a line on the fifth of the scale gives a sense of resolution, but it's not as strong a resolution as the root note. That's why we'll only use it to end some of the lines in this solo. When you start making up your own licks, end them on either the root note or the fifth of the scale to make your solos sound more complete.

Example 6 combines the last two examples and adds a new ending in measures 6–8. To pull this off, lift your index finger off the first string after you play the first beat of measure 6. When you bring it back down again on the third beat, barre the first and second strings at the fifth fret by pressing down both strings with the fleshy part of your index finger. Play the E note that ends measure 6 and you're already in position to play the A in measure 7, which gets held for the full measure. Play that same note again in measure 8, then the half rest gives you a moment to get your hand in position again.

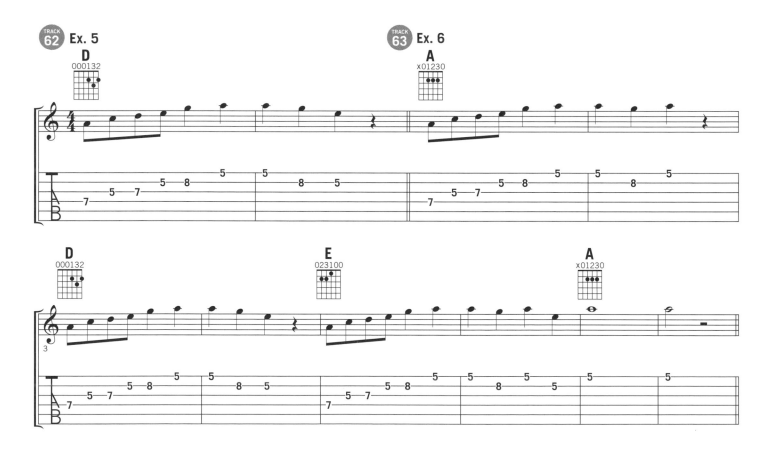

Get Ready for the Descent

Notice the rhythmic similarity of **Example 7,** which is a descending scale, to Example 4. Even when the notes are different, a rhythmic theme gives you something familiar to work with in your solo. Once again, you have a rest at the end of measure 2 to find your footing for the next line.

If you play Example 7 but change the last two notes, ending on the E at the fifth fret of the second string, you'll have **Example 8**. Just like in Example 5, by ending on this E, you're landing on the fifth, which resolves the lick and adds variety to your solo so you're not constantly landing on the root.

Now, back to back, play Example 7, Example 8, and then Example 7 again. All you need to do to get **Example 9** is add that little closing lick. Once you do, you have an eight-measure descending solo.

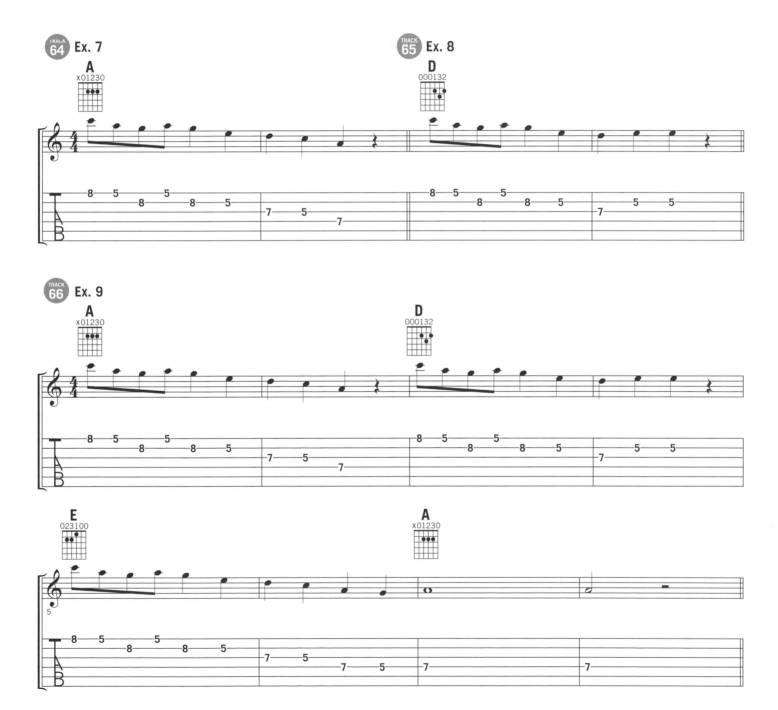

Up 'n' Back

Music by Jason Garoian

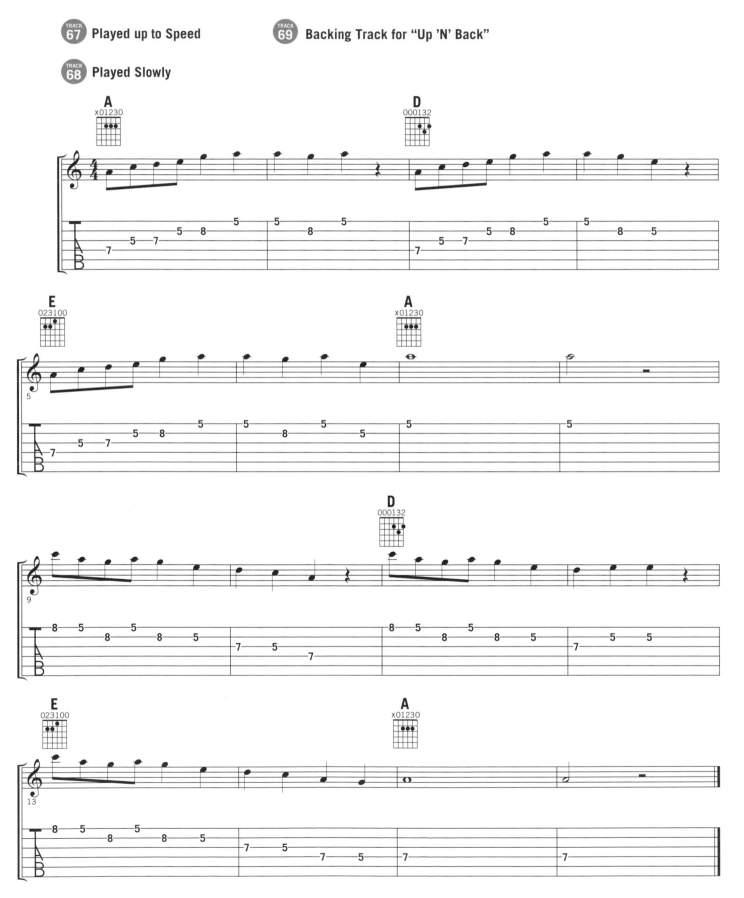

Bring It All Together

Now, play it all together as **"Up 'n' Back."** You've got a complete solo, ascending, descending, and ending on the root note, which brings the whole thing home.

Once you're comfortable playing it slowly, play it over the backing tracks on the CD to see how it works over variations of the I–IV–V–I chord progression. Once you get really fast and can play it at about 200 bpm (100 bpm in 2/2 time), try it over the chorus of "Lay Down Sally."

You just used notes from the minor pentatonic scale and some rhythmic variation to create a solo. Nice work! Now, use those tools to come up with your own lead lines. Remember: the root and the fifth are safe notes to end on, but mess around with other notes to see what sounds good to you.

Serious Soloists

Listening to masterful solos can fill you with inspiration, fueling you on your journey. They also broaden your musical vocabulary and illuminate what is possible with the guitar. Here's a short list of some heavyweight players who could solo like no one before them:

JIMI HENDRIX. Gifted with a deep musical background and a wizard-like ability to bend feedback to his will, Hendrix forever changed the world of rock guitar solos.

DICK DALE. Dick Dale blew the doors off surf rock in the '60s, playing with invention and a soaring technical facility.

KURT COBAIN. Cobain's solos used scales, but he transcended their confines by allowing intuition to guide his playing in the pioneering grunge band Nirvana.

DJANGO REINHARDT. Even though two fingers on his fretting hand were severely burned, Reinhardt played beautiful melodic runs at lightning-fast paces, and today his name is synonymous with Gypsy jazz.

Bonus Backing Tracks

 D–A–E–A Chord Progression   A–E–D–A Chord Progression

ADVICE FOR
BEGINNERS

Guitar Shopping

What are the different types of guitars, and what kinds of music are they used for?

The guitar family can be sliced and diced and categorized in many ways, and to confuse matters further, there are numerous instruments that straddle categories. The most basic distinction is between guitars that use steel strings and those that use nylon strings.

In North America, **steel-string guitars** are the ones we most often see and hear. The most common acoustic variety (i.e., guitars that make music just fine without cords or electrical current) is the **flattop guitar,** which crops up in countless styles from traditional folk, blues, and country on down through contemporary unplugged rock. Typically built with a hollow wooden body and a round soundhole and patterned after the historic designs of the C.F. Martin and Gibson companies, the flattop guitar is what people usually mean when they say **acoustic guitar**. Although any type of guitar can be electrified, the term **electric guitar** almost always refers to a solid-body steel-string instrument with one or more magnetic pickups; these guitars (the archetypal forms being the Fender Stratocaster and the Gibson Les Paul) are once and forever associated with rock 'n' roll, although they are used in many other genres as well.

Less common types of steel-strings are **archtop guitars,** which take their key design traits from violin-family instruments (f-shaped soundholes, arched tops). Archtops began as acoustic instruments, and some are still built that way today, but they are usually played plugged in, producing the mellow, muted sound that we think of as jazz guitar.

Also in the steel-string family are **resonator (or resophonic) guitars**. These guitars have interior aluminum

headstock — inlay — tuning machine — nut — fret — position marker — fingerboard — neck — heel — upper bout — soundhole — waist — rosette — pickguard — saddle — bridge — bridge pin — lower bout — soundboard

Acoustic Flattop Guitar

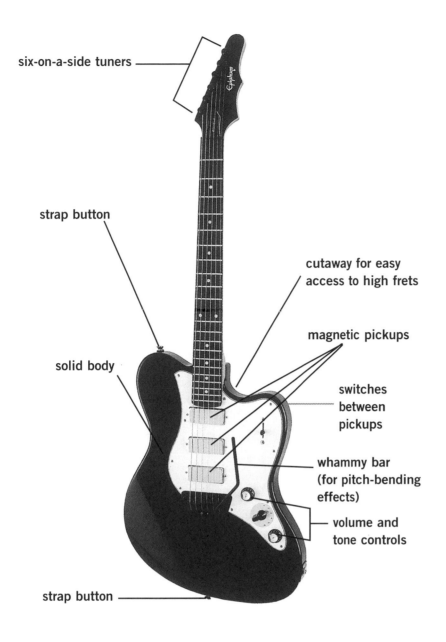

six-on-a-side tuners

strap button

cutaway for easy access to high frets

magnetic pickups

solid body

switches between pickups

whammy bar (for pitch-bending effects)

volume and tone controls

strap button

Electric Guitar

Godin's Multiac, with a thin, hollow body and MIDI capabilities, is one of many contemporary acoustic-electric hybrids.

cones that amplify the sound like a loudspeaker does and create a unique sustaining tone. Some resonators are built with metal bodies, others with wood; some are played like regular guitars, while others sit flat across your lap (or are held in a similar position by a strap) and are played exclusively with a slide—the so-called **Hawaiian style**. These instruments are often referred to by their dominant brand names, **National** and **Dobro,** and have strong associations with blues (especially the metal-body ones) and country/bluegrass (especially the wood-body Dobros played with a slide bar).

While steel-strings rule in North America, **nylon-string guitars** are dominant in most of the rest of the world. Most common is the **classical guitar,** an acoustic instrument defined by Spanish makers in the 19th and early 20th centuries. Some people call classical guitars **gut-strings,** a reference to the material used for strings before the adoption of nylon in the '50s. As the name suggests, these instruments

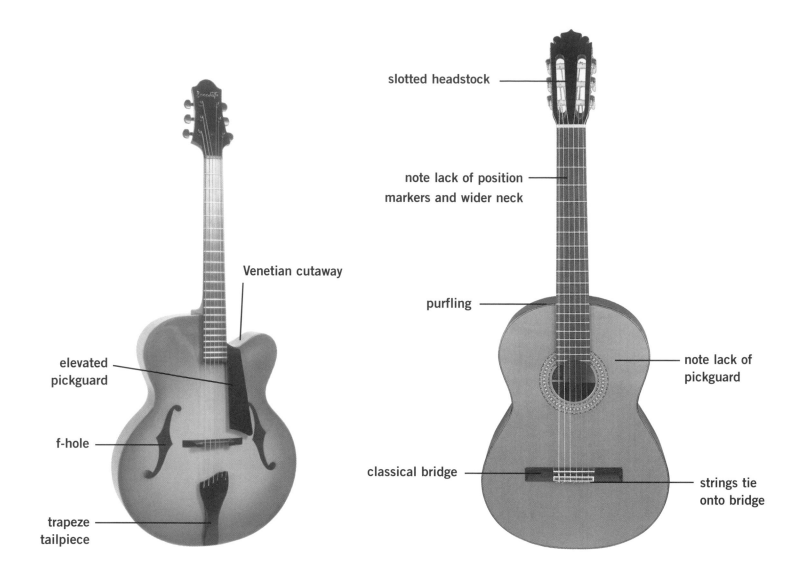

slotted headstock

note lack of position
markers and wider neck

Venetian cutaway

purfling

elevated
pickguard

note lack of
pickguard

f-hole

classical bridge

strings tie
onto bridge

trapeze
tailpiece

Archtop Guitar

Classical Guitar

are traditionally used for classical music and plucked with the fingers (though that never stopped Willie Nelson from battering his old nylon-string with a pick!), and they have wide, flat fingerboards that facilitate classical technique. Nylon-string guitars of this type also are used extensively throughout Latin America for all sorts of indigenous styles.

Flamenco guitars are similar to classicals but are constructed more lightly and from different woods (traditionally cypress for the back and sides rather than rosewood for a classical guitar), and they often have violinlike **friction tuning pegs**. Flamenco guitars usually have a plastic plate (***golpeador***) to protect the top from the tapping techniques used in flamenco music, and their strings are set up closer

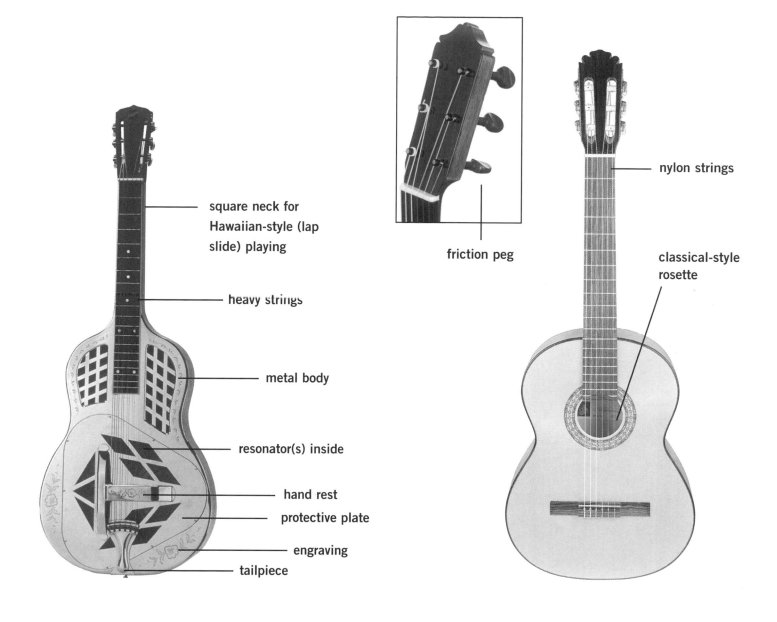

square neck for Hawaiian-style (lap slide) playing

heavy strings

metal body

resonator(s) inside

hand rest

protective plate

engraving

tailpiece

friction peg

nylon strings

classical-style rosette

Resonator Guitar

Flamenco Guitar

to the fretboard to create an edgier, more percussive tone. These instruments are not often found outside flamenco and the strains of world music it has influenced.

In recent years, amplification technology has inspired new forms of the nylon-string guitar with thin or solid bodies and skinnier necks similar to those found on steel-strings, and these hybrids have in turn found a home in more and more styles of nonclassical music. We now have solid-body instruments designed to sound like acoustic instruments when plugged in, and hollow-body instruments that use amplification to sound like electric guitars. Confused? The guitar family tree keeps growing new twigs and branches, presenting players with an amazing array of options.

Is it better to start out with an acoustic or an electric guitar?

Among teachers, there is a pretty strong consensus that it's best to start with an acoustic because it forces you to focus on the fundamentals of technique and sound. It's just you and your guitar, without all the distractions of wires and boxes and amps, which require an entire learning curve of their own. When you play an electric guitar, you are essentially playing the amplifier and the effects pedals as much as you are playing the guitar itself.

Jimmy Tomasello, who teaches guitar and plays in various rock, R&B, and funk bands in the Chicago area, recommends that people start with acoustic guitar even if they ultimately want to play electric. "It is more responsive and more controllable," he says. "One needs to work on dexterity before [addressing] the tone issue of the electric." Since acoustic guitars generally have thicker necks and heavier strings than electrics do, they require more muscle and better technique at the outset. "If you can get a good acoustic tone," he says, "you'll be totally slammin' when you plug in." If, on the other hand, you start on an electric and then pick up the acoustic later on, you will likely have a much harder time building the necessary strength and chops.

Is learning the acoustic steel-string completely different from learning classical guitar?

In many respects, yes. The differences start with the instruments themselves. The string materials sound and feel radically different: Steel strings are sharper, louder, and more aggressive sounding, while nylon creates a softer, more melodious tone. Thin steel strings temporarily dig painful grooves into the fingertips of beginners, while nylon strings are fatter and gentler, which is why classical guitars are typically recommended for kids and sometimes for older beginners. Standard classical guitars have wider necks than steel-strings do, which makes for tougher left-hand stretches but in the long run makes possible the kinds of intricate finger-work that define classical guitar music. Traditionally, classical guitars are played with the guitar resting against a left leg elevated by a **footstool**, again to facilitate the kind of movement around the neck required in classical music; by contrast, steel-string players hold their guitars sitting and standing in all sorts of idiosyncratic positions—virtually every way except the classical position with a footstool. Classical players carefully maintain long right-hand fingernails for plucking the strings; some steel-string players do this too, but many more simply use a pick or their bare fingers and never worry about their nails.

The differences go deeper, down into the way the instruments are taught. Classical guitar teachers emphasize reading music, learning composed pieces, and mastering strictly controlled techniques, while teachers of the steel-string, with its roots in folk and rock, are much more apt to focus on playing songs by ear. The former lays a foundation for a long road of learning, while the latter offers more instant gratification. There are many points on which a classical- and a folk- or rock-oriented teacher will disagree, right down to the "correct" position of your hands. These are all sweeping generalizations, of course, but the fact is that nylon- and steel-string guitars offer very different sounds, and they are separated by a cultural, pedagogical, and technical divide.

Guitarists making the switch from one instrument and approach to the other need to make many adjustments. Those steeped in classical studies will probably find their strong technical foundation to be an advantage on the steel-string. But they also may have trouble starting to improvise and play by ear, just as steel-string players switching to classical may struggle with written notation and learning by rote. Ben Harbert, a classical player and former head of guitar teaching at the Old Town School of Folk Music in Chicago, points out that "much of classical guitar uses open chords or pieces of open chords. Classical students who have some experience with steel-string styles can take a lot of the left hand over to classical. Also, the steel-string student achieves success early on, granting an element of confidence when beginning classical. On the other hand, guitarists are often intimidated by classical studies. Many of my classical students become burdened by correcting bad habits that they developed learning another style: the left-hand thumb position (thumb poking up and above the guitar neck), the right hand plucking across the strings rather than pushing the strings down into the body of the guitar . . . I could go on."

The traditional classical playing position, with footstool.

If you haven't played either instrument and are trying to make a choice, you should follow your gut response to the sound and repertoire of the guitars themselves. "Students should learn the music that interests them," says Harbert. "Most people follow paths from genre to genre. Often a student will become interested in another style that warrants a new instrument: for instance, going from Black Sabbath to Randy Rhoads to classical guitar, as many guitarists did in the '80s."

Finally, keep in mind that it is entirely possible to play jazz or folk or new age or whatever style on a nylon-string, just as it is entirely possible (though less common) to take a more formal, classical approach to the steel-string. So if you are attracted to the sound of one instrument but the repertoire of another, you can choose a less-traveled path.

What should I consider in choosing between a straight acoustic and an acoustic-electric?

In recent years, amplification systems for acoustic guitars have gone from being an option to being practically standard equipment. In many cases, manufacturers have simply added pickups to their existing acoustic models, and the acoustic properties of the instruments are not affected by the retrofitting. But many other instruments are designed from the ground up with amplification in mind, and they strike a compromise between acoustic and electric sound: they tend to be thinner bodied and have less unplugged volume, but they can sound great plugged in and be more trouble-free on stage.

So your choice really hinges on whether the acoustic or amplified sound is more important to you. What do you see yourself doing with this instrument, now and down the road? Margie Mirken of Shade Tree Stringed Instruments says that from her perspective "the most important things are tone and playability, so a pickup system takes a backseat. If a student thinks it's fun to plug in and make a big sound even before he or she is ready to get a gig, so much the better. Have a blast. But I also see people who've bought a really bad guitar (bad tone, back neck angle, bad frets, horrible playability) with a pickup system, and it's apparent that the manufacturer put all the money into the electronics. The student is really loud but sounds terrible."

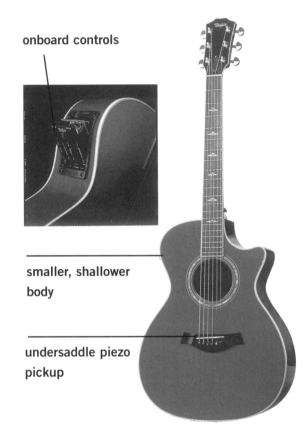

onboard controls

smaller, shallower body

undersaddle piezo pickup

Acoustic-Electric Guitar

In the end, you are buying a guitar first and a pickup system second, and you need to make sure the guitar is a good one that you can grow with. Keep in mind that pickup systems can be very easily and inexpensively added to acoustic instruments, so if you are not sure you want or need to plug in, you should get the best straight acoustic you can and see how your interests develop over time. Also remember that amplification technology is changing constantly. Acoustic-electric guitars with built-in pickup systems, especially those with control panels cut into the side of the instruments, commit you to the current technology, so you may be better off with a system that can be added, removed, and upgraded as your needs change.

Yes, you might need to buy a left-handed guitar, and yes, you might do fine playing a regular righty model. Remember, playing the guitar isn't like handwriting or throwing a baseball; you need *both* hands to make music on the thing.

So try a regular right-handed model for awhile, and see how it feels. Your two hands are being asked to do very different tasks: the right hand carries the rhythm and drives the sound by strumming or picking, mostly using large motor coordination of the arm, while the left makes smaller, more precise finger movements between strings and frets. In a way, this is a logical division of labor for a lefty, because the dominant hand is assigned the more sophisticated task, which also requires more strength, at least in the fingers.

But that doesn't change the fact that for some southpaws, playing this way will just feel *weird*. You may really want to strum those strings with your left hand, no matter how many times you try it the other way. If this is true for you, by all means make the switch. Unfortunately, you can't simply flip the guitar over to play lefty, because the strings are then in the opposite order: the ones with the lowest pitch (the bass strings) are now down closest to the floor, while the highest strings are up toward the ceiling. Although a few guitarists have bucked tradition and made great music this way (notably Elizabeth Cotten, who wrote the folk classic "Freight Train"), a flopped-over guitar literally turns conventional technique upside down: you play treble notes with your thumb and bass notes with your fingers, rather than the other way around. If you play upside down, good luck—you won't find much help from any teacher or book!

When shopping for a lefty guitar, you may find a few options in your local music store, but don't feel limited by what's on the rack, because many models can be special-ordered in left-handed versions. It is also fairly easy and inexpensive for a repairer to convert a righty guitar to a lefty by changing the nut and (on a steel-string guitar) the saddle to accommodate the reverse string order.

I am left-handed. Do I need to buy a special lefty guitar, or should I learn to play a regular model?

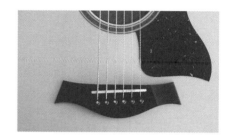

Notice how the string order and angle of the saddle are reversed on these righty (top) and lefty models.

Trying to discern the differences between guitars separated by hundreds or even thousands of dollars on their price tags can be tricky, especially for a newcomer to the instrument. Modern factories are very skilled with cosmetic details, so that even very inexpensive guitars can look downright fancy. Complicating matters further is the fact that as you move up the price scale, the objective differences in quality from one guitar to the next diminish, and the judgment about which one is better becomes much more a matter of personal preference.

In the extremely competitive field of guitar retailing, prices are always in flux and often negotiable, but we can draw some rough guidelines about what you'll find in different ranges.

Under $500

Guitars in this budget category are produced in large batches in factories, and their across-the-board quality has notched up in recent years—great news for beginners. Also great news is the fact that steel-string guitars in this price range are now available in a few body sizes, whereas in the past almost all were large, dreadnought-sized instruments, which can be tough going for smallish players.

What's the difference between a $200 and a $2,000 acoustic guitar?

One of the defining features of guitars in this budget category is the use of **laminated woods** (multiple, very thin sheets of wood glued together, as in plywood) rather than **solid woods** like those found on higher-end instruments. Laminates are stable and easy to work with in the factory, and guitars made with them can sound good. But all-laminate guitars don't have the tonal character of solid-wood guitars, which are renowned for the way the sound opens up over time as the instrument gets "played in." Above $300 list or so, you will begin to find guitars with solid tops (usually spruce) and laminate backs and sides (rosewood, mahogany, and other woods), which are a significant step up in quality from all-laminate guitars—not just because of the top, but because these instruments usually get better materials overall and they also might come with essentials like cases and warranties. You can sometimes spot a solid top by looking at the edge of the soundhole: if it's solid, you'll see the grain lines running all the way through the top; if it's laminated, the grain lines will be broken (see drawing below).

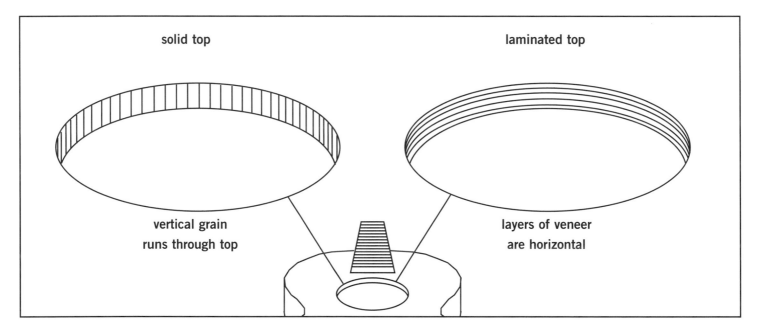

solid top

laminated top

vertical grain
runs through top

layers of veneer
are horizontal

If you can swing it with your budget, by all means go for a solid-topped model, which is more likely to continue satisfying you tonally over the years and is built to last. Scoring a solid top in this price range usually means skipping some frills and cosmetic touches, like decorative inlays and a high-gloss finish, a trade-off that is well worth making. Ditto for budget models with pickups: you're better off with a straight acoustic model if the manufacturer has skimped on the fundamentals in order to include the electronics.

One of the most persistent myths about factory guitars is that they are identical down to the last detail. It ain't so—hands and machines collaborate on building all guitars, and each piece of wood is different, so a rack of instruments of the same model from the same factory will vary in construction quality, tone, and playability. This is especially true in this price range, where the quality control is not as strict as in more expensive guitars. So look and listen closely, and engage the help of someone with experience to determine if the particular guitar you are interested in is well constructed and can be adjusted, now and tomorrow, for smooth and easy playing.

$500 to $1,000

Just a few years ago, this was a fairly unpromising price range, mostly filled with gussied-up versions of imported budget instruments. But along came a computer revolution in guitar manufacturing, which has allowed factories everywhere to turn out basic versions of their much more expensive models for unprecedented low prices. In the late 1990s, North American companies broke the $1,000 price barrier for all-solid-wood guitars, a sonic boom that echoes across the guitar market today.

When you reach this price range, you should expect the guitars to be well made, with clean construction and a higher grade of materials, and protected by hard-shell cases and limited lifetime warranties. Like solid-topped guitars under $500, all-solid-wood guitars under $1,000 are likely to be relatively plain compared to their more expensive brethren. But instruments like these represent an incredible opportunity for players to own guitars fundamentally like those that used to be available only for $1,500 and much more. If you start out with a budget instrument but later want to upgrade, it makes a lot of sense to aim for this all-solid-wood threshold.

In the under-$1,000 range you'll also find good-quality guitars made from a combination of laminated and solid woods, as well as acoustic-electric instruments (some full-size, some thin-body) with sophisticated pickup systems that make great stage guitars. Usually these guitars feature easy-access tone and volume controls on the upper bout of the guitar, which can be very handy but mean that your guitar has a large hole cut in the side that will be there forever. So if you are getting an on-board amplification system like this, make sure you want it.

$1,000 to $2,500

Once you are up into four figures, you can pick from a wide range of professional-quality guitars built in factories with all solid woods. List prices for top models by famous names like Martin and Gibson will run higher—sometimes way higher—than $2,500, but these companies offer plenty of options in this range. Stan Jay of the venerable music store Mandolin Brothers in Staten Island, New York, says that the quality of these instruments is reflected in all stages of their manufacture. "All processes are performed at a high level, from the layering of lacquer, continuously buffed out, resprayed, and buffed again, to the selection of wood **purflings** [the strips of wood around the edge of the body], to the shadings and the stainings, to the installation of precision componentry. It should certainly approach flawless work. The sound should be lush, the sustain palpable."

The difference between the $1,200 model and the $2,400 model becomes a matter of materials and appointments—the cheaper one might have a lower grade or different type of wood, satin rather than gloss finish, plain dot fingerboard markers rather than elaborate inlays. Upper-end amplification systems also add substantially to your cost. As with any consumer product, intangible factors like brand reputation and perceived value definitely affect how guitars are priced. Sometimes there is less difference from one to the next than meets the eye or the ear of even an experienced player. If the cheaper one delivers for you, tonally and aesthetically, go for it.

Over $2,500

You'll still find large-factory guitars at prices from here on up to the stratosphere for limited editions and such. But you'll also find a greatly expanded universe of options, which includes instruments from small- and medium-sized shops (e.g., Collings, Santa Cruz, and Lowden) and the army of individual **luthiers** out there designing and building guitars on their own.

"A $3,000 acoustic guitar," says Stan Jay, "would be favorably compared to the guitars of the major makers that were made during their **'vintage'** period, a time when procedures were followed or woods were chosen that are no longer routinely available in those factories. The golden era for the acoustic guitar was 1929 to 1946. For electrics, it was 1949 to 1969."

At this level, practically anything can be customized—for a price, of course. In contrast to the factory assembly line, instruments in this range are built with quite a lot of attention to the characteristics of specific pieces of wood and how they work together in a particular guitar—trained hands make subtle adjustments to get the most out of each guitar. Especially with individual makers, attention is also paid to your particular needs and desires as a player, not just for custom visual details but for your playing style, preferred strings, and planned uses for the instrument (home, stage, studio).

So back to the $1,800 question: Is a $2,000 guitar *that* much better than a $200 guitar? Well, yes. The pricey instrument is definitely more refined and probably quite a bit easier to play; its sound has more depth and nuance and will improve over time, and if cared for properly, it will last for at least a lifetime. The budget guitar sounds as good now as it will ever sound, and it won't survive nearly as long as the boutique model. But if the $200 or $300 guitar gets you on your way as a player, that's the most important job an instrument can ever do. And when you are ready to move into an instrument with more potential—and you will know when that moment has arrived—many great guitars await you.

What sizes of guitars are available, and how can I tell if an instrument fits me well?

There are a few size factors that you should be aware of as a guitar shopper. First and most obvious, there is the body size—a primary consideration for acoustic instruments. In steel-string guitars, beyond downscaled instruments for kids and travelers and the occasional "baby" models (some of which are tuned higher than standard tuning), you'll find an array of standard sizes including, from smallest on up: **parlor, concert** or **0** (pronounced "oh"), **grand concert** or **00** ("double oh"), **auditorium** or **OM/000** ("triple oh"), **grand auditorium, dreadnought,** and **jumbo.** Toward the smaller end of the spectrum falls the standard classical guitar body. The way these and other terms get tossed around in the guitar world may make your head spin (just try figuring out what is meant by "small jumbo," for instance!), but what is more important than a model's history or anatomy is the way it feels and sounds in your arms.

The powerful, hefty dreadnought has been the standard flattop guitar for many decades, but this is not a situation of one size fits all. "If you get a small man or small woman or a younger person and hand them a dreadnought," says veteran performer and teacher Carol McComb, "it can be impossible for them to actually play it. It's too big to reach around and play without having to hold it in some really odd, awkward manner. Most women who are small look dwarfed by a large guitar."

Pay attention to how your right arm and shoulder feel as you reach over the guitar and down to the strings, a function of both the dimensions of the top and the depth of the sides. Comfort is essential; contorting your body will not only make it harder to play, it may injure you in the long run. "The more experienced player will instinctively know, by trying many examples, what size feels right," says Stan Jay. "A novice may not immediately know, but trial without time pressure is recommended." Ergonomic considerations aside, different body sizes offer different sonic possibilities, and you may find yourself over time gravitating from one to another, or acquiring a couple of instruments of varied sizes. In my own case, over a couple of decades I've gone from dreadnought to bassy jumbo to trebly grand concert to something right in the middle as my ear and playing ability have developed.

Standard Acoustic Body Sizes

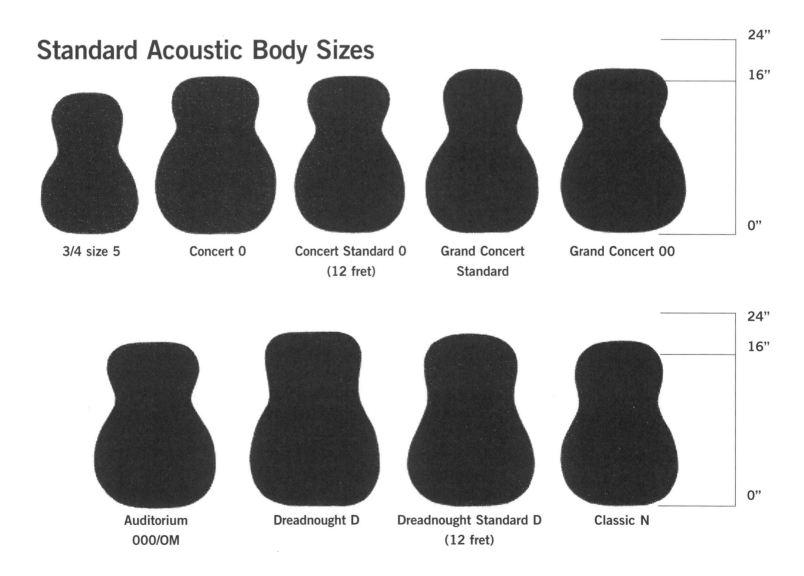

| 3/4 size 5 | Concert 0 | Concert Standard 0 (12 fret) | Grand Concert Standard | Grand Concert 00 |

| Auditorium 000/OM | Dreadnought D | Dreadnought Standard D (12 fret) | Classic N |

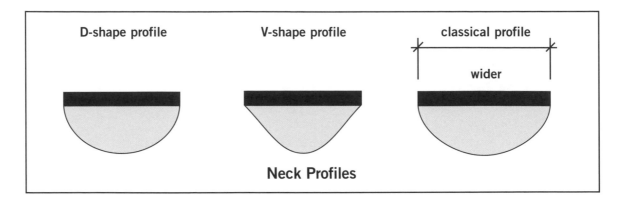

Neck Profiles

The other important size considerations relate more to your fretting hand. The neck shape (or **neck profile**) will vary considerably from model to model—if you cut a bunch of necks in cross-section (see drawing above), some would look rounded (like a D), others more pointed (like a V); electric guitars and acoustics adopting their characteristics have much thinner necks than traditional acoustics do. The **scale length,** or vibrating length of the string, affects your reach from fret to fret as well as the tension you feel on the strings (a longer scale length will generally feel harder to play). The **fingerboard width** is an important factor too, because it affects how far apart the strings are, which in turn affects what you do with both hands. Classical guitars have wider fingerboards (typically two inches wide) than steel-strings, which are often in the range of $1\frac{3}{4}$ to $1\frac{11}{16}$ inches. Does that tiny fractional difference in width really matter? It does, although as Margie Mirken points out, "Whatever you start on will feel normal." People with big hands don't necessarily need guitars with fat fingerboards, but if you chronically feel as if your fingers are battling for space down on the fretboard, you might try out a model with wider string spacing for a while and see if it makes a difference. It's worth noting that fingerstyle (as opposed to pick) players tend to prefer wider necks, so your technique can be a factor too.

In any case, the key to finding your way through all these options is pretty simple, not to mention pretty entertaining: play lots and lots of guitars. A shop with a diverse selection and a nonpressured atmosphere will greatly streamline the process of finding the right fit.

One of the toughest things in guitar shopping, especially for a beginner, is recognizing what are fatal flaws in an instrument—problems that are either unrepairable or too expensive to repair given the value of the guitar—and what aspects of how it feels and plays are easily adjustable in the course of a routine setup.

Let's take the latter category first. Setup work, which will be described in more detail in the next chapter, addresses several aspects of the guitar's sound and feel, but of particular significance to you is the action: the height of the strings off the fingerboard. High action makes it more difficult to press the strings down to the fingerboard, so you generally want the action to be as low as possible without causing the strings to buzz. The other major factor is the strings themselves—lighter-gauge strings will ease the work of your fingers. So if you love everything else about a guitar (the look, the tone, the price) but find it harder to play than others, see if a lighter set of strings might make the difference. The same goes for a guitar with a buzz problem: it might be easily fixable. Old, dirty strings will keep a guitar from staying in tune and remove all of the sparkle from the sound, too; don't hesitate to ask for a new set if the guitar you're checking out sounds really dead. The need for small adjustments like these should not deter you from buying a guitar—they are standard procedure and should be part of your purchase.

What are the most important structural flaws to look for when checking out a new guitar?

Then there are the flaws that should make you put that guitar right back on the rack. "In the fatal category," says Stan Jay, "incorrect **neck angle** (usually when the action's too high and there's no way to lower it) is the most common and least remediable flaw." Other less-common problems on his list include: a wavy fingerboard, uneven frets, insufficient play in the truss rod, unstable top (look out for bulges or depressions), off-center strings, and bad **intonation** (i.e., notes up the neck that sound out of tune).

One way to check the intonation is to learn to play a harmonic at the 12th fret: while lightly touching (not pressing down) a string with your left hand exactly over the 12th fret, pick the same string with your right hand. When you hit it just right, you should hear a chiming tone that continues even when you take your finger away from the string. On each string, compare the 12th-fret harmonic to the note you get when you press down the string at the same fret. If these two notes do not sound in tune with each other, the guitar has an intonation problem.

Your best insurance against these flaws is simple: choose a good shop in the first place. "A well-run guitar shop will not wait for the customer to discover such guitars," says Jay. "Each incoming guitar should follow a specified check-in procedure, and any that do not meet the 'implied warranty of merchant-ability' rule should be pulled out and returned to the manufacturer. They should never see the showroom floor."

Where's the best place to shop for a guitar—the local shop, the music superstore, the Internet?

For researching a guitar purchase, the Web is a useful tool; just about every manufacturer has extensive photos and specifications available at the click of a mouse. But as a shopping medium, it leaves a lot to be desired. You might be able to look at a picture of the instrument, but that's not the same as seeing it in person and holding it and hearing it. Even if you have done hands-on investigation and decided on a maker and a model, buying it online is a risky proposition, because there will be differences—sometimes significant ones—from one example to the next. Getting a good setup is an essential part of buying a guitar, too, and the online retailer usually leaves you to commission this work separately.

So until the day comes when you can download a demo guitar from the Web, you should buy your instrument in the real-time, physical world. Let's take a look at what an ideal shop would be like, whether it's a mom-and-pop outfit or a chain superstore. It would have a wide but carefully selected array of instruments, reasonable prices, knowledgeable salespeople who don't start counting their commission when you walk in the door but who give you the time and space to think clearly, quiet rooms where you can play instruments as long as you like, a respectful attitude toward women shoppers and beginners of all ages, an active repair shop with a reputation for good warranty and nonwarranty service, and a teaching studio in case you want lessons.

The point is, though, that the place you buy your guitar is very important. In fact, going to a good shop substantially increases the odds that you'll wind up with an instrument that is right for you. Even if you know exactly what you want and can save a few bucks bargaining across town, you may wind up spending the difference and more on "extras" like setup work and a new set of strings—things that the other shop would throw in for free. A relationship with a good music store will be valuable to you as long as you play the guitar—long after the "deal" you cut is forgotten.

That's not to say that good deals cannot be gotten from music stores. But when you are shopping in an environment where the salespeople are clueless or untrustworthy (or when you're on the Web and essentially on your own), you've really got to know what you want, what you're looking at, and what it's worth. You've got to be able to spot the guitar with a neck that is at such a low angle that it will soon develop a permanent, unfixable buzz (a good shop will actually put a lemon like this right back into a box marked "Return to Sender"). You've got to have a clear enough sense of your own preferences that you won't be talked into a different model that just happens to bring the sales guy a higher commission. In other words, a good music store allows you to relax and make your decision in an unhurried, unstressful, and confident fashion.

So you are ready to buy a guitar—you have done some thinking and research about the basic types of instruments and narrowed the field; you have found a music store or two that carries the kinds of guitars you're interested in; and you've got some money saved and have set a preliminary budget for yourself (including some allowance for lessons and instructional materials). Here are some tips on how to complete the process.

Be patient. "Give yourself time to try out a lot of guitars," says Mark Dvorak, a guitarist, banjoist, and teacher at the Old Town School of Folk Music. "I think it's important to feel that the decision to buy has not been rushed. If you are already enrolled in lessons or a class, you might feel an urgency to pick out an instrument right away. Borrowing a playable instrument is a cheap solution. And renting a playable instrument is money well spent, in my opinion, even if you wind up renting for an extended period of time.

"If the guitar is to become a part of your life, you and your instrument are going to be spending a lot of time together. Students who spend a month or two or six trying out a dozen or more guitars and listening to what people have to say about different models will put themselves in a good position to select an instrument they will be happy with over the long haul."

Along the way, watch out for salespeople who hit you with any variation of the opening line, "Are you planning on going home with a guitar today?" Needless to say, their commissions and sales targets, and not your long-term satisfaction, are foremost in their minds. Don't let them push you into a hasty decision.

Get recommendations. You will find that advice is very easy to come by. Guitar magazines and music websites offer a steady stream of information, reviews, and new product announcements. Friends and acquaintances will be happy to offer their opinions, and online forums are packed with people who are just dying to tell you exactly which guitar to buy. Online discussions can be useful because they pull together people of similar interests from all over the place, but then again, you don't have any idea who the individuals behind the screen handles are. Beware of those who seem intent on trashing one brand and putting another on a pedestal. Think of yourself as a political pollster, and pay more attention to general trends in what people recommend than in a single person's (especially a stranger's) opinion.

And don't make your decision solely on these third-party recommendations. Instead, use them to help you draft a list of guitars to try for yourself and to give you a general idea about what they might cost.

Bring along a helper. The key to making the right decision is confidence, and if having a friend along increases your comfort level, definitely bring one. Many guitar teachers will help students choose an instrument (it is worth at least knowing that in some cases, teachers receive a commission from a music store for their referral—but if your teacher is straightforward and trustworthy, this arrangement shouldn't cause any particular conflict of interest).

Margie Mirken recommends that beginners bring a helper along, but she cautions that "many fairly experienced players don't know anything about guitars, either, so don't let them make the decision for you." Also don't bother bringing along someone who plays in a completely different style from what you are interested in

What's the best way for a beginner to shop for a guitar? Should I get help from a teacher or a friend?

(e.g., a classical player wouldn't be much help in trying out electric guitars) or who steers you toward these cool $1,500 guitars rather than the $400 models you actually are considering.

Practice a few try-out songs. If you can play at least a little, practice a few songs, chord progressions, or picking patterns so that you can play them smoothly and unself-consciously in front of others. In addition to playing chords, advises renowned guitar teacher and author Frederick Noad, "it is worth learning in advance how to play single notes, so as to be able to try the high reaches as well as the low positions." Not only will a little rehearsal put you more at ease in the store, but it will mean that you are comparing apples to apples—you'll be playing the same pieces on a series of guitars and hearing how each one responds. If you strum one guitar with a pick, fingerpick the next one, then play a little lead on the next one, you will have very misleading ideas about how they compare.

Hearing someone else (your helper or one of the salespeople) demo the guitars can be instructive too, especially if you are just starting to play.

Look as well as listen. Obviously you want a guitar that sounds good, with all the structural features discussed above. But looks matter too, even though you may run across players who insist they don't. The ideal guitar for you, as bluesman Steve James once put it, "makes you feel like playing every time you so much as look at it."

Watch for hidden costs. Be savvy about prices and get the best deal you can, but consider the factors that lie behind the price tag. Is a setup included? A new set of strings, picks, a capo? What are the store's return policies? What kind of warranty or repair support will you get? Some inexpensive guitars come with manufacturers' warranties and others do not, but often what matters to you more than the piece of paper from a distant corporation is the service you get from the place where you actually bought your guitar.

The good news for shoppers today is that there are many well-made, attractive, inexpensive instruments available with a lot of music in them. You are not looking for a needle in a haystack—you're looking for one of a number of guitars that will be very satisfying for you to own and play. If you've done your homework, taken your time, and feel a strong attraction to a guitar you can afford, take it home. Congratulations.

Equipment Basics

A **setup** is a series of adjustments to your guitar that keep it playing and sounding its best. Guitars are not static objects—over time the forces of climate, string tension, and playing make small but significant changes in factors such as the **action** (the height of the strings from the fingerboard), which, in turn, dramatically affect how your guitar sounds and feels. A setup might fix something as obvious as a loudly buzzing string or do something as subtle as making barre chords a little easier to play.

So a guitar setup, best done at a professional repair shop, is not unlike the 30,000-mile checkup for your car. The difference is that a new guitar probably needs a setup even before you take it home for the first time. Guitars are given a general setup before being shipped from the manufacturer, and a shop may tweak them further before hanging them on the rack. But a good setup involves optimizing a specific guitar for a specific player, and that can be done for you only with your input.

The things most commonly adjusted during a setup are the nut, the saddle, and the truss rod. Let's take a look at what these are and how they might be attended to during a setup.

The **nut** is the piece of bone or plastic that your strings rest on at the headstock end of the fingerboard; it has small notches cut in it for each string. If the nut is too high, you will have a much harder time pressing down the strings, especially in the first couple of frets. One good test of whether your nut is too high is to put a capo at the first fret (for a full explanation of the capo, see the last question in this chapter). If your guitar feels much easier to play with the capo, your nut probably needs to be lowered, which the repair shop accomplishes with a little filing or sanding. Sometimes strings can get caught in the nut slots, which causes tuning problems and can also be fixed with some quick filing.

The **saddle** is the piece of bone or plastic (on an acoustic), or metal (on an electric), that the strings rest on at the other end of the guitar—on the bridge. Repairers often raise (or **shim**) the saddle a little bit to fix a buzz, and sand it down a little bit to lower the action. It's important that the saddle be at a height where it can be raised or lowered; a saddle that is teetering too high or has been ground down very low doesn't give the repairer much room for adjusting anything and is a red flag for a big problem. Other common adjustments to the

What is a guitar setup, and what is adjusted during this process?

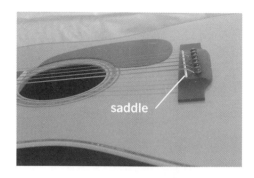

saddle

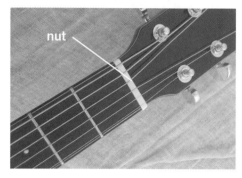

nut

saddle include filing it to improve the intonation (i.e., to make it play more in tune all the way up the neck) and smoothing out a sharp spot that causes the same string to break repeatedly.

The **truss rod** is a metal rod that runs through the middle of the neck of almost all steel-string guitars and can be adjusted to keep the neck straight. Adjustments are made either through the soundhole or beneath a small cover plate on the head-stock, with small turns of an Allen wrench. While it might be tempting to try adjusting the truss rod yourself, don't do it unless you really know what you are doing and why you are doing it. It is far too easy to misdiagnose the problem (maybe the truss rod is fine and something else is out of whack) or to turn the truss rod too far or in the wrong direction.

Like any other kind of maintenance, guitar setup is an ongoing process. Not only does your guitar change over time, but you do too, and a new development in your playing style might alter your setup preferences. Switching to heavier or lighter strings may necessitate some setup adjustments. If you want to play slide, your action might need to be a tad higher to get a decent sound. If you start tuning down the bass strings a lot for alternate tunings, you may find that the strings buzz too much and the saddle needs to be raised on the bass side. And so on. The way to keep up with all these changes is to cultivate a relationship with a good repairer and to take your guitar in for periodic maintenance, just as you do your car.

Adjusting the truss rod with an allen wrench.

Aside from my guitar itself, what pieces of equipment will I need?

At the top of any list of accessories has got to be strings. Without them, your guitar might look nice but will be pretty darn quiet, and you will want to keep an extra set on hand for when they break or go dead. To set those strings ringing, you'll need some picks, unless you plan to play with your right-hand fingers. And to help you keep the strings in tune, you will want some sort of tuning device; these days, electronic tuners are inexpensive and ubiquitous, although a tuning fork will also do the trick. If your guitar didn't come with some sort of case or bag, you should get one; you could get by without it, but you are asking for dings and trouble if you are planning to take your ax with you anywhere. And where else are you going to put all the other accessories that you are now accumulating?

Optional, but very handy, is a **string winder**, a gizmo that spins your tuning pegs much more quickly than your fingers can and speeds up the process of changing strings. String winders usually include a little plastic piece for pulling out steel-string bridge pins, a task that can be tough otherwise. To complete your string-changing kit, you will also need some small clippers (wire cutters, not fingernail clippers) to cut off the extra ends of strings. And do your guitar a favor and throw in a nice 100-percent cotton cloth for periodic wipe-downs of the strings and body. All of the items just mentioned will be discussed in more detail in the remainder of this chapter.

You may want to use a strap to hold your guitar in position—you definitely need one if you want to play standing up. On an acoustic guitar, you may have to get a repair shop to install an **endpin** or **strap button** for attaching the strap on the butt of the guitar (all electrics, and many acoustics, come with endpins already installed). On an acoustic guitar, the other end of the strap can tie onto the headstock, or you can get a strap button installed where the neck meets the body so your strap fits snugly over your shoulders. Classical players have their own accessory for holding the guitar in the traditional playing position: a footstool that elevates the left leg for the guitar to lean against, or else a small frame device that sits on your leg and performs the same function but allows you to keep both feet flat on the floor.

A string winder speeds up string changes considerably.

For electric guitarists, of course, the list continues. At a bare minimum, you will need a cord (with quarter-inch jacks at both ends) and some kind of amplifier to plug it into. Most likely you will also want to have an effects box of some sort, which requires another cord and either a battery or an AC power supply. And then another box, and then another box . . .

A plethora of picks and pedals.

There are actually fewer differences between strings than meet the eye. In fact, most of the string brands vying for your attention on the rack are made by just a handful of manufacturers, so there are greater variations in packaging and marketing than in actual string technology.

Your guitar was designed to use either steel or nylon strings. **Steel strings** have a steel core wire, and the bottom (lowest-pitched) four strings are wound with some sort of metal as well. **Nylon strings** have a nylon core, and the bottom three strings also have metal windings. You can't really put steel strings on a guitar designed for nylon strings or vice versa—the one made for nylon strings would collapse under the much greater tension of steel strings, and the one designed for steel strings would sound pretty wimpy with nylon. The way steel and nylon strings attach to the guitar is also different, as you'll see in the next question. (The one exception to all this is a set of **ball-end nylon strings**, which can be put on a steel-string guitar, with varying sonic results.)

With steel strings, the main difference from one brand to the next is in the alloy used for the winding (brass, bronze, phosphor-bronze, etc.) and the size of the winding and core wire. Some brands are also coated to extend string life and give you a smooth feel under the fingertips. Within each brand you'll find a variety of **string gauges**—this refers to the thickness of the string, measured in hundredths of an inch. Sets are generally identified as (from thinnest to thickest) **extra-light, light, medium-light,** and **medium gauge**. (There used to be such a thing as heavy gauge, but virtually nobody uses them

I am a little overwhelmed by all the choices of strings. What are the important differences between them?

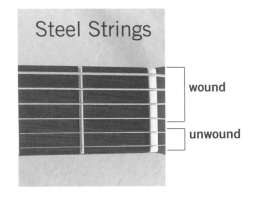

Steel Strings

wound

unwound

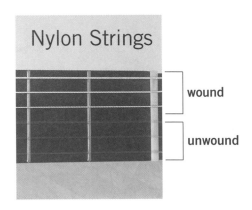

Nylon Strings

wound

unwound

anymore, and for good reason—these are the kinds of strings referred to as "bridge cable." So today's medium strings are really the heaviest strings you can buy.)

The typical light-gauge set of acoustic steel strings has gauges from .012 on the first string to .054 on the sixth (the shorthand for this in guitarese is just to say the gauge of the first string, as in, "I use 12s on my Taylor"). A typical medium-gauge set goes from .013 to .056. Is that difference of .001 or .002 significant? You bet. Medium strings may pull more sound out of your guitar than lights, but they also put more tension on it—in fact, excessively heavy strings can seriously damage a guitar, so follow any guidelines you receive from a shop or manufacturer about what gauge strings to use (or not to use). Medium-gauge strings also require more muscle from you. As a rule, beginners should use light strings; Some players recommend trying out **silk-and-steel strings**, which are even lighter and easier on tender fingers. As you gain strength and experience, you may want to try other gauges to find the best match for your style and your instrument. String gauge is a less complicated issue for electric guitars, because they are pretty much always strung with lights or extra-lights to facilitate string bending, and any loss in volume can be easily compensated for with the turn of a knob.

With nylon strings, you won't see designations for light and medium gauge, etc. Instead, string packages will be marked as **extra-low, low, normal, hard,** and **extra-hard tension** or something similar. Coated nylon strings are available, as are sets with wound rather than plain third strings and other special features. Some sets (both steel and nylon) are polished to reduce the squeak that inevitably happens when you slide your fingers up and down a wound string.

As you shop for strings, you will hear a lot of talk about which brands are "brighter" or "warmer" or "more brilliant." These are subjective terms, to say the least, so judge for yourself how strings sound and feel. Just start with a reasonably priced set of whatever your shop recommends, and if you are so inclined, experiment with other gauges, brands, and types the next time your strings need to be changed.

What's the best way to change strings?

Ask ten guitarists how often they change their strings, and you'll get probably as many answers: every few weeks, once a year, every couple of months, before every gig, only when strings break, never . . . Many factors affect the decision to put on a new set, from the amount you play to how hard you play to your disposable income to your laziness level to simple personal preference—new strings have a crystalline clarity that a lot of people like but others dislike. Professional musicians, who are playing constantly and need consistently high performance, tend to change strings frequently. There is a major physiological factor too: some people's hands produce acidic sweat that kills all the sparkle in new strings before they've even played through one song. Coated strings can help this common problem, and they will last longer regardless of what your sweat glands are like.

In other words, you have to find the string-changing schedule that works for you. Pay more attention to whether your strings still sound good and are working properly than to how much time has passed; as the late folk bluesman Dave Van Ronk once said, "When God wants you to change strings, He has a way of letting you know." Old strings sound dull and muffled, and they become hard to tune. And they weaken and break. If you've got a fairly old set and break a string, you may as well replace all six, because one lively new string will sound weird amidst a bunch of dead ones. Note, however, that nylon-string players often replace the wound bass strings more frequently than the unwound trebles, which last a long time. Some manufacturers address this need by packaging nylon-string sets with extra bass strings.

Now onto the matter of how to change strings, a pretty simple operation once you've done it a few times.

Changing steel strings

Step 1: Take off the old string(s). Contrary to popular belief, it won't hurt your guitar to remove all six strings at the same time if you are changing the whole set (if your guitar has an undersaddle pickup, though, this may not be advisable, as it can lead to balance problems). This is an opportunity to give your whole guitar, fingerboard and all, a good cleaning. To remove the string, you first turn the tuning machine until the string is nice and slack, and then you pull out the bridge pin. If you have a string winder with a little notch for pulling out pins, use that. Otherwise use your fingers or your string clippers, being very careful not to scratch the guitar or the pin. (Note: On electrics and some acoustic guitars, the string simply slides through a hole in the bridge rather than being held by a bridge pin. If this is true of your guitar, loosen the old strings, then cut them in half with your clippers, slide the old strings out and the new ones in, and move on to Step 3.) After the string is free on the bridge end, you can detach it from the tuning post.

Use a string winder to remove bridge pins.

Step 2: Put a slight bend in the string down near the ball end; this will help the ball end slip into position under the bridge. Slide the ball end of the string down into the hole, followed by the bridge pin, with its hollow side facing toward the soundhole. Give a little tug on the string; the ball end should be lodged against the underside of the bridge, not hanging on the end of the bridge pin.

Step 3: Slide the other end of the string through the hole in the tuning post (see image A, below). Leaving a small amount of slack on the string over the fingerboard, loop the free end back around the tuning post (toward the inside of the headstock) and under itself (image B), then bend it over to lock the string into position (image C). (Note: This description assumes your steel-string guitar, like most of its brethren, has a **solid headstock**, with the tuning posts sticking straight up and the tuning knobs on the side. A few acoustic steel-strings, however, have slotted headstocks similar to those found on classical guitars. If this is the case with your guitar, follow Step 3 in the nylon-string section below.)

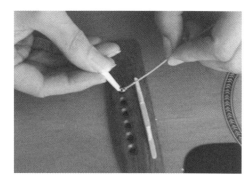

Ball end of the new string goes through the bridge, followed by the bridge pin.

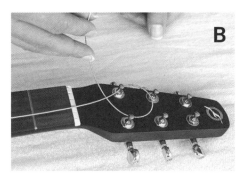

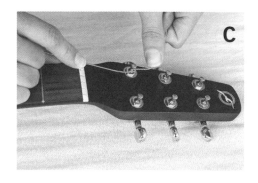

Notice on the left-hand headstock that the two rows of tuners turn in opposite directions. On the right-hand headstock, they all wind in the same direction.

Step 4: Tune the string up to pitch, sending the string around the inside of the post first (see photo at left). A string winder will make the process go much more quickly. The fewer times the string wraps around the post, the better. If you've left the right amount of slack in Step 3, the string will wrap only once or twice around the post by the time it's in tune.

Step 5: With your clippers, cut off the extra string. These little sharp string ends that remain can really gouge you, so make them short. Bend the ends down with the side of the clippers, just to be extra safe.

Changing nylon strings

Step 1: Remove the old string by turning the tuning peg until the string is loose and can be untied easily from the tuning post and the bridge.

Step 2: Tie the new string to the bridge. Classical guitar strings do not have ball ends to hold them in place, so you need to secure them with a simple loop. Push one end of the string through the hole in the bridge (see image A, below). If you're changing

 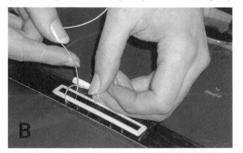

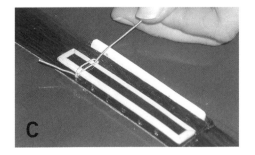 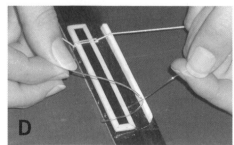 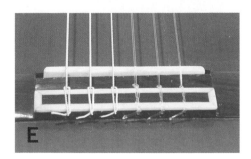

a wound string and it has one flexible end with loose windings, use this end. Loop the string back around and under itself just behind the saddle (image B, previous page), then thread it under itself one more time at the back of the bridge (image C, previous page). You can also put one more loop in the string before securing it at the back of the bridge; a common practice is to use this double loop for the unwound treble strings and a single loop for the wound basses (image D, previous page). Clip off the extra string, leaving a short tail (image E, previous page).

Step 3: Attach the string to the tuning post. Leaving a small amount of slack on the string over the fingerboard, thread it through the hole in the post (image A, below). Loop the free end back around and under itself (image B), then through the loop you just made to make it secure (image C).

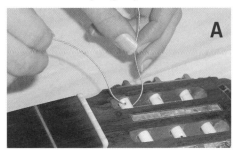
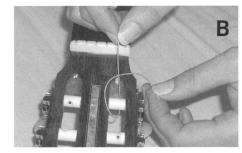

Step 4: While holding the loose end of the string with one hand so the loops don't unravel, tune the string up to pitch. As with steel strings, the string should wrap around only once or twice by the time it is in tune. As you are tuning up, try to guide the string so that it wraps around the post toward the outside—this will help keep the strings away from each other.

Step 5: Using your clippers, cut off the ends of the strings down near the tuning posts.

Stretching

New strings take time to stretch—nylon strings may not even settle in for several days. As strings stretch, they fall in pitch, so you will need to keep tuning them back up until they stay there. You can accelerate the stretching process a little bit by giving a gentle tug on the string at around the 12th fret, then tuning back up. Do not yank hard on your string, though, because you'll wind up with a string that is kinked or stressed and impossible to tune.

Now the work is done, so enjoy your new strings. Fresh strings and a good polishing can give your guitar—and you—a whole new lease on life.

There are four basic types of cases offering quite a wide range of protection (from very little to practically gorillaproof) and cost (from $20 on up to more than you probably paid for your guitar).

The most basic case, and the one that traditionally comes with a budget guitar, is made of chipboard, which is like a heavier form of cardboard. Shops refer to these as **soft-shell cases**. If you have an inexpensive guitar and only need a case to stow it away at home and carry it around locally, a soft-shell case will do fine. Don't expect it to do much other than keep your guitar from getting scratched; it offers minimal protection from impact.

What kinds of cases are available?

Higher-end guitars come with hard-shell cases.   **Guitar to go: the gig bag.**   **For serious traveling: the flight case.**

Moving up a notch in quality and security are plywood **hard-shell cases**. Pricier models have thicker wood and are arched on the top and back for better impact protection, and their latches and handles are sturdier. Many high-quality guitars these days come in molded plastic cases, which are a lighter-weight alternative to plywood cases. Whether ply or plastic, these kinds of cases will protect your guitar from small bumps and some rough handling, but they are not adequate for serious traveling.

At the high end are **flight cases**, which are designed to help your guitar survive the rigors of baggage handlers and the road. These are expensive, heavy duty, and just plain heavy but are considered essential equipment for traveling musicians with fine instruments.

By contrast, **gig bags** provide only padding for the guitar rather than a rigid shell. In return you get very light weight and great portability—you can sling your guitar right over your shoulder or carry it like a backpack. There is a huge range in level of protection and price for gig bags, from basic nylon exterior and little or no padding to swanky leather and thick foam. Gig bags are made for carrying your guitar around town, not for traveling. Since a gig bag takes up much less room than other kinds of cases, it is tempting to carry your guitar onto a plane in one of these for easy stowing in the overhead compartment. But if a flight attendant forces you to relinquish your guitar to baggage, you are going to be very sorry you don't have a hard case.

Obviously, the quality of case you should get rises with the quality of the guitar, and the more traveling you do, the better case you will need. No matter what kind of case you choose, it should fit snugly around your guitar without putting pressure on any of the guitar's parts, and it should support the neck. The latches and the handle should be strong and reliable—believe me, you do not want your case to open up accidentally as you are walking down the sidewalk with it. And a case should feel natural and comfortable to carry.

What do I need to know about protecting my guitar from heat, humidity, scratches, and dirt?

In taking care of your guitar, a little common sense goes a long way. Keep your guitar in a safe place where it will not get knocked over by kids or dogs or someone fumbling for the door in the dark, and preferably store it in a sturdy case with all the latches closed so you won't inadvertently pick up the case and deposit your guitar on the floor. If you use a guitar stand, buy a good one that will not tip over easily, and find a place for it away from foot traffic. Don't go straight from eating a plateful of greasy french fries to playing your guitar—wash your hands and save your strings. Keep jewelry, zippers, and big belt buckles away from your guitar, because all can leave scratches in the finish.

Aside from these sorts of household hazards, the most important factors in your guitar's welfare are temperature and humidity—both have a dramatic effect on the structural stability and playability of wooden instruments. "Keep away from extremes of temperature," says Stan Werbin of Elderly Instruments in Lansing, Michigan. "I would say try to avoid prolonged exposure to temperatures under 50 or over 100 degrees Fahrenheit." That means keep your guitar out of the chilly basement and away from radiators and heating vents as well as intense direct sunlight, whether indoors or out. If you hang your guitar on the wall, avoid the outside walls of the building. An extremely common guitar killer is the trunk or back of a car, which on a sunny summer day can do serious damage within a short period of time. Imagine yourself in the guitar's position; only leave your guitar in places where you yourself would be comfortable.

Humidity is a subtler though no less important consideration. Your regional climate is a major variable—a guitarist in bone-dry Arizona faces different issues from someone in sticky Florida—although many places experience high humidity on muggy summer days and low humidity during the winter when central heating dries out the indoor air. "Always keep your guitar well humidified," says Werbin. "At home, if possible, use a house or room humidifier that keeps the humidity between 40 and 50 percent. Don't trust cheap gauges to measure humidity, since they are notoriously inaccurate." If your room or house is too dry, or if you are going away from home for an extended period of time, a soundhole **humidifier** (available at music stores) will keep your guitar in good shape, although you need to be careful not to overhumidify or spill water on it. Watch your instrument: if your guitar is too dry, the top may sink and the strings may start to buzz on the higher frets, while excessive humidity may make the top bulge out and the action too high. For high humidity, a room dehumidifier or a silica gel pack in the case will keep moisture in the normal range.

A lot of these problems are alleviated, or at least lessened, by keeping your guitar in a good hard-shell case, which acts as a buffer against the environment. If you transport your instrument through subzero weather and then bring it inside a toasty house, leave the guitar in its case for a few minutes to warm up slowly. If you open it right away, you might be greeted with an ugly crack in the finish.

Secure those latches before you hit the road.

Pad the headstock before you fly.

A good case, of course, also protects your guitar from many of the hazards of traveling. That is, except human ones—keep your guitar with you as much as possible to avoid theft.

Airline travel is a source of major anxiety for musicians, and with good reason, given all the instruments that are battered, cracked, stolen, and lost every day somewhere between the plane and baggage claim. Try to carry your guitar on board with you, but don't be surprised if you are intercepted by a flight attendant. Be polite but firm in pointing out that your guitar will fit in the overhead bin (and hope that this is, in fact, true!); minimize your other carry-ons so that you don't look like a space hog. Even if you are forced to hand over your guitar (and on little commuter planes you have no choice), you are probably better off having checked it at the gate, where it doesn't have to negotiate the baggage maze. Ask to pick it up at the other end right when you get off the plane, although regulations may prevent you from doing this.

The odds of your guitar emerging intact from the baggage hold are greatly increased by a heavy-duty case. No matter what type of case you have, loosen the strings before you go on board (this might keep the peghead from snapping off if your case takes a big hit) and pack some T-shirts or other soft clothes under and on top of the peghead, just to give it extra support.

Finally, a word about cleaning your guitar. For most everyday dirt, a simple wipe with a soft chamois cloth or old cotton T-shirt is all you need. Wiping off your strings after each playing session will lengthen their life. For more stubborn dirt on the body of the guitar, first try breathing a little moisture onto the dirty spot and then wiping it off; if that doesn't work, use one of the guitar cleaners available at the music store. Over time, grime will build up on your fingerboard. Once in a while (maybe once a year), when you are changing strings, you can gently clean the fingerboard with very fine (0000 grade) steel wool. Add a tiny dab of lemon oil if you like, wipe off any excess, and your guitar is ready to go.

What is the difference between using a flatpick, fingerpicks, and your plain old fingers?

Let's sort out the terms first, because they can be baffling. First we have the triangular-shaped **flatpick**, also known simply as a pick or (in millions of dusty old method books) as a **plectrum**. No matter what word you use, you hold a flatpick between your thumb and index finger and strike the strings with it. Flatpicks are the driving force in all sorts of guitar music, but, confusingly enough, people often use the term flatpicking to refer specifically to bluegrass guitar technique.

Fingerpicks are metal or plastic extensions for your index, middle, ring, and sometimes pinky fingers that give them a lot more power in attacking the strings. They are almost always accompanied by a **thumbpick**, which similarly turbocharges the thumb. (A thumbpick is not, however, always accompanied by fingerpicks—many players, following the example of Chet Atkins, use a thumbpick and bare fingers.) Fingerpicks find their most common use in country blues and folk. Again, just for a little confusion, **fingerpicking** doesn't necessarily mean using fingerpicks—it just means using your fingers instead of a flatpick. (Sorry! I didn't come up with these terms.) **Fingerstyle** is used pretty much interchangeably with *fingerpicking*.

Each of these little devices has its pros and cons. The flatpick is a rhythm machine, great for strumming and percussive grooves and for getting lots of noise out of your guitar, plus it is the tool of choice for most modern lead-guitar styles. The main limitation of the flatpick is that it has only one point of contact with the strings; by contrast, if you use your fingers, you can have four or even five appendages working on different strings simultaneously. So the fingerstyle approach opens up a lot of technical and musical possibilities, although by dropping the pick you give up a lot of easily accessible volume and power. You can develop those things playing fingerstyle, but it takes considerably more finesse.

Playing with fingerpicks feels quite different from using your bare fingers. With fingerpicks, your fingers are further away from the strings. You get lots of volume—in fact, maybe too much, because it is hard to control the clatter and get a good tone. If you go with the bare digits, you have yet more choices: you can maintain longish fingernails (or apply artificial nails), as most nylon-string players and many steel-string fingerpickers do, or you can simply use the pads of your fingertips.

As you can see, there are quite a few options when it comes to something as basic as deciding how to hit the string—that's one of the keys to the guitar's versatility. Many guitarists wind up using more than one technique or develop a hybrid (a common one being **pick and fingers**—holding a flatpick and then fingerpicking with the middle and ring fingers). The good news is that experimenting with various types of picks is cheap and fun. Your choices include not only flatpicks vs. fingerpicks vs. no picks but all the many materials and gauges (thicknesses) of picks available today. Trying different possibilities is certainly a lot easier on the wallet than buying different guitars!

Take your pick: a flatpick (above) and thumb- and fingerpicks.

What is a capo, and how do you use one?

A capo is a slick little device that presses down all six strings of the guitar at whatever fret you choose. There are several designs, from simple elastic bands that wrap around the neck to various ways of clamping and holding a bar down across the fingerboard (in a pinch, you can even try the traditional homemade version with a pencil and a thick rubber band!). Guitarists will go to their graves arguing for the inherent superiority of one model over another, but no matter—all capos perform the same basic function.

And that function is to raise the pitch of all the strings by the same amount without your needing to retune them. If you attach the capo at the first fret, for instance, your open strings now ring a half step (the interval of one fret) higher in pitch. If the capo is at the second fret, all the strings are a whole step (two frets) higher—your normal tuning of E A D G B E is now magically raised to F♯ B E A C♯ F♯. And so on up the neck.

So why would you want to clamp such a thing on your unsuspecting guitar? For several very good reasons. The main one is to accommodate the range of your singing voice. Let's say you are singing a song in the key of A and accompanying yourself with A, D, and E chords, but the melody is a bit low for your voice. You could put a capo at the second fret, hold those same chord fingerings, and sing comfortably, because the melody is now a whole step higher. You are actually playing in the key of B—the capo has raised your A to B, your D to E, and your E to F♯, even if you don't know how to play an F♯ chord on your own! Neat trick, eh?

Take a look at the chart (on the next page), which shows what chords you get when you play the five most common open chords with a capo at various positions

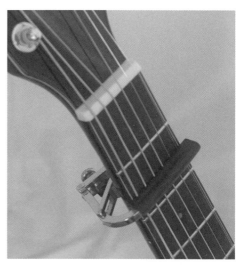

This capo is holding down all the strings at the second fret.

up the neck. Only the first seven frets are listed, because capos are rarely used higher than that.

No capo	Fret 1	2	3	4	5	6	7
A	A#/B♭	B	C	C#/D♭	D	D#/E♭	E
C	C#/D♭	D	D#/E♭	E	F	F#/G♭	G
D	D#/E♭	E	F	F#/G♭	G	G#/A♭	A
E	F	F#/G♭	G	G#/A♭	A	A#/B♭	B
G	G#/A♭	A	A#/B♭	B	C	C#/D♭	D

All those sharps (#) and flats (♭) may make your eyes a little bleary, but remember that as far as your fingers are concerned, you are still playing the five familiar chords in the first column; the capo does the work of transforming them into the other chords listed.

In addition to adjusting the key to make your voice or someone else's more comfortable, you might use a capo to play along with another instrument. Let's say your pal likes to sing and play a song in the dreaded key of F—you could capo at the first fret and play a nice, easy E fingering. Capos are used in a lot of recorded music, so putting one on might also help you play along with a CD.

The capo also gives you the option to play the same chords at a different place on the neck and therefore get a different sound. An example: You could play G, C, and D chords without the capo in the usual way, but you could also put a capo at the fifth fret and then play D, G, and A fingerings that will sound as G, C, and D. Chord positions up the neck like this have a distinctive flavor—just think of the sweet little guitar part in "Here Comes the Sun," which we owe not only to George Harrison but to his capo (he capos at the fifth fret and plays D fingerings that sound in the key of G).

Finally, there is one fringe benefit to the capo for beginners: it tends to make your guitar's action a tad lower, especially when you capo on the first few frets, so the strings become a little easier to play. Nothing wrong with easing up on the finger calisthenics from time to time.

Getting in Tune and Getting Started

There are two paths to getting your guitar in tune—using a tuning device and using your ears—and both are essential. For a beginner, a device like an electronic tuner is a godsend: it helps you over the initial hurdle of getting in correct tune, and it also initiates the longer and no less important process of training your ears to know instinctively when a string is or is not quite in tune.

Before we run through a few good methods and tools for tuning, let's check the notes that we are actually tuning the strings to. The notes of **standard tuning** on the guitar are, from the lowest-pitched string to the highest:

String	6	5	4	3	2	1
Note	E	A	D	G	B	E

The way you tune the strings, of course, is by turning your **tuning pegs** (which are, by the way, also referred to as **gears, tuning machines,** or just plain **tuners**); one direction raises the pitch, the other lowers it. No matter what tuning method you use, always tune a string *up* to the target pitch— the tuning will be more stable that way. That means if the string is tuned a little too high, you should drop it below the note you want and then raise it slowly back up.

Electronic tuners

These battery-powered devices listen to the sound of an individual string and indicate on a meter of some sort (usually lights or a needle) whether the note is higher than, lower than, or right on the desired pitch. Electronic tuners pick up the sound through either a small built-in microphone or a direct feed from an electronic pickup—you plug your guitar cord right into the tuner. Some models attach temporarily onto the body or headstock of the guitar and "read" the pitch from the vibrations rather than from the air, which works much better than a mic in a noisy room. The exact way that tuners function varies from model to model—on some, you need to flick a switch to tell the tuner which string you're tuning, while "hands-off" models take care of that automatically. The simplest guitar tuners read only the notes in standard tuning; more expensive **chromatic tuners** can read any note, which is a handy function if you ever get into alternate tunings or want to check your tuning while using a capo.

These days, for the truly wired guitarist, there are software tuners that function similarly to stand-alone electronic tuners—you plug into your computer to check your tuning. These programs have the advantage of being able to play

What's the best way to tune my guitar?

This basic tuner reads the notes of standard tuning.

notes through MIDI files, and some offer sophisticated functions for alternate tunings.

Electronic tuners are found in just about everyone's guitar case—they're cheap and easy to use, and onstage or in some other noisy environment, they provide just about the only feasible way to tune. Pitch pipes, which used to be standard guitar-case accessories before electronic tuners, can go out of tune themselves, and besides, they don't tell you whether you are in tune or not. The one caveat about using an electronic tuner is that you should not shut off your ears. "It is easy to be kind of mindless and just look at it—'Oh, it's in the middle, so it must be in tune,' and move on to the next string without actually getting involved in the process," says guitarist and teacher Carol McComb. "You need to listen if you're trying to develop your ears. Tuners are very good biofeedback tools, if you pay attention to them and listen to the note and think, 'Do I think this is in tune? And does the machine think this is in tune?'"

Keep in mind that tuners show only a very small variation above and below the target note. So if your string is way off, the tuner won't give you a useful reading. You have to get the string in the neighborhood of the correct note, then fine-tune it using the tuner. For that reason, it's a good idea to have a tuning fork even if you've got an electronic tuner—it will give you a note you can hear and sing for getting in the ballpark of the correct pitch.

Tuning fork

If you are not using an electronic tuner, you will be mostly relying on your ears and fingers to tune up your guitar. But unless you are blessed with perfect pitch (i.e., you can sing a dead-on A note out of the blue), you will need some way of knowing that at least one of your strings is in correct tune. Once you have that, you can tune all the others in relation to that one string.

The **tuning fork** is one simple, portable tool for finding that reference note. You just hold it by the stem down near the knob end, knock the prongs against something hard like a guitar case (not, please, your guitar), then, while letting the prongs vibrate, rest the knob on the top or bridge of your guitar, which will produce a clear, loud tone. Most guitarists use an E tuning fork, which matches the open first string; another option is **A 440** (440 hertz, that is), which is considered the standard reference pitch for all music and corresponds to the note at the fifth fret on your first string. After you tune one string correctly, follow the fretted-notes method below to tune the other strings.

If you have trouble hearing whether the string is higher or lower than the pitch of the tuning fork, try singing or humming the two notes. The higher note will feel higher in your throat.

What's On Top?

One endless source of confusion is all the ways people refer to their strings (high, low, top, bottom, first, sixth . . .). Here's a rundown of seven ways to describe those six strings of yours.

E	A	D	G	B	E
Sixth	**Fifth**	**Fourth**	**Third**	**Second**	**First**
Thickest . . . . Thinnest
Lowest pitch . . . . Highest pitch
Bottom. . . . . Top
Low E. . . . . .High E
Bass. . . . . Treble
Closest to ceiling. . . . . .Closest to floor

The important thing to remember is that most of these terms refer to the pitch. That is, your **"high E"** or **"top"** string is the highest-pitched one, and your **"low E"** or **"bottom"** string is the lowest-pitched one. That makes sense, as long you don't get hung up on the fact that the "high" or "top" string is actually the closest to the floor, while the "low" or "bottom" string is closest to the ceiling.

There is one other string-related oddity you should know about. Tunings are always listed from the lowest-pitched string to the highest (E A D G B D), yet the strings are numbered from the highest-pitched (1) to the lowest (6).

If you can just commit these things to memory, as counterintuitive as they may seem, you'll save yourself a lot of headaches while reading lesson books or communicating with other guitarists.

A tuning fork held against the bridge produces a clear, loud tone.

Piano

You can get all six of the pitches you need from a piano, as shown in the diagram. I would recommend, however, using a piano for only one reference pitch—just hit an A on the piano and tune your fifth string to it. Then tune up all the other strings in relation to each other, away from the piano. That way, you won't get thrown off if the other piano keys are slightly out of tune, and besides, even under the best circumstances,

it is difficult to get a guitar and a piano to sound exactly in tune with each other.

Fretted notes

Here is the simplest way to tune up without an electronic tuner. First, you should get a reference note from a tuning fork, a piano, or another instrument. Let's begin here by tuning your first string to an E note, but you could start with any of the other strings.

As you may have noticed, your first string is not the only one tuned to E—your sixth string is too, so let's go to that one next. These strings are tuned in octaves, which are simply occurrences of the same note at different frequencies. The sixth-string E is two octaves lower than the first-string E. It's pretty easy to hear when octaves are in tune, so play the first and sixth strings back to back and adjust the sixth to match the first. (For an even slicker way to tune the sixth string to the first, see the harmonics section on page 78.)

Now onto the other strings. When your guitar is in tune, with one exception, each open string matches the note you get at the fifth fret on the string below it in pitch. So, for example, the fifth string matches the note on the fifth fret of the sixth string. The exception is that the second string matches the note on the *fourth* fret of the third string. Take a look at the fingerboard diagram and you'll see how this pattern goes.

So let's use this information. Once your sixth string is in tune, you want to play it at the fifth fret and match the open fifth string to that A note. Does the fifth string sound higher or lower? If it's lower (flat), raise the pitch by tightening the tuning peg slightly and then rechecking the note. If it's higher (sharp), loosen the string by turning the tuning peg in the other direction. If you are not sure which way you need to go, try moving up and down the frets on the sixth string: if, when you play the sixth string at frets one through four, it sounds like the note is closer to the open fifth string, then you need to tune the fifth string higher; if, when you play the sixth string at fret six or higher, the pitch sounds closer to the fifth string, then you need to tune down.

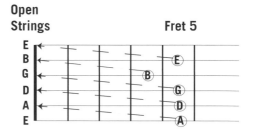

Follow the same procedure for all the other strings. The fifth fret of the fifth string matches the open fourth string, the fifth fret of the fourth string matches the open third string, the fourth fret of the third string matches the open second string, and if all has gone according to plan, the fifth fret of the second string now matches the already-tuned first string. If not, you need to go back and recheck the whole chain of tuning, starting with your reference note and string.

When two strings are in tune, the fretted note and the open string are in **unison**—the pitch is the same. When two strings are close to the same pitch but not quite, you will (if you listen very closely) hear something usually referred to as beats—a subtle pulsing that results from the way the sound waves rub against each other. When the two notes are in unison, the beating disappears—it sounds smooth and even. Try listening for these beats and using them to help you home in on the right note.

Octave check

Octaves provide a good way to check the results of the fretted-notes method. Not only do you have E notes on the open first and sixth strings, but you have one on the second fret of the fourth string as well. So you can check that all these notes sound in tune with each other, and do the same thing for other notes and other strings.

Here is a series of octaves that you can check for each open string.

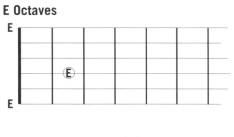

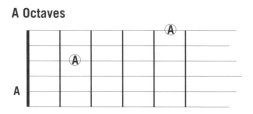

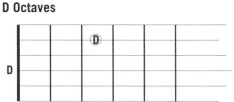

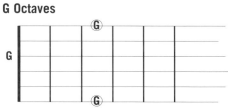

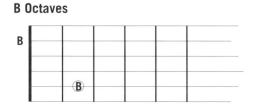

Harmonics check

Here is one last way to check your tuning. A **harmonic** is that nice, chiming tone you get by lightly touching a string directly above a fret (not pressing it down against the fingerboard) and picking it with your other hand. It's a magical sound, and it can be useful for fine-tuning your strings. The diagram to the left shows some harmonics and the fretted notes you can check them against.

Last but not least, try the one at the bottom of this page. It's harder to get fifth-fret harmonics to ring than 12th-fret ones, but keep micro-adjusting the placement of your finger on the string and eventually you'll find the sweet spot.

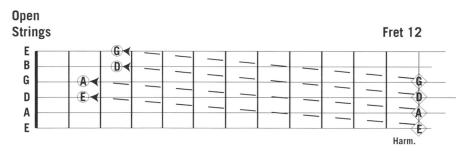

As mentioned above, if you tune your first string to a tuning fork, you can use this harmonic to tune the sixth string, then use the fretted-notes method to tune strings five, four, three, and two.

If you try out a few of these tuning methods, you'll find that some are easier for you to hear and use than others—it's an individual thing. Start with an electronic tuner; and when you're comfortable with that, try tuning one string with the tuner and then the rest by ear with the fretted-notes method. Your ears, after all, do not require batteries, and training them well is an investment that will pay off as long as you play music.

This, unfortunately, is one of those rites of passage for everyone learning the guitar—especially the steel-string variety. Your fingertips, which have led a pretty cushy life to date, suddenly find themselves having to press against thin wires, sometimes for hours at a time, and they will complain bitterly about their new assignment. But yes, the pain will diminish as your fingers toughen up and calluses develop, probably in a matter of weeks or a few months, so hang in there. In the future, you may go through this experience again if you take a hiatus from the guitar or if you significantly notch up the time and intensity of your playing, but it probably won't hurt as much as developing your first set of calluses.

There are a few tips that might ease the pain in the meantime. One is using lighter-gauge strings: lights are much softer to press down than mediums, and silk-and-steels are even softer still. Coated strings, though more expensive, also do not dig into your fingertips as hard as regular strings do. Another consideration is action: if your strings are higher off the fingerboard than they need to be, some inexpensive adjustments might really help (see the setup discussion in Equipment Basics on page 63).

Pace yourself while you play, too. Short, daily practice sessions are better for building calluses than one marathon a week. Usually what hurts the most is holding the same chords down for very long periods of time, so switching over to a different song or exercise might give you some relief. Don't push yourself too hard, and definitely give it a rest if you feel pain in your hand, wrist, or arm, which could be a sign of a more serious problem.

As a guitar player, you need to be more careful about your fingers than you probably were in the past. Keep harsh solvents and cleaners away from your skin—use rubber gloves. Also, don't play guitar when your fingertips are waterlogged. Wear rubber gloves while you do the dishes, or else just give your fingers time to dry and harden before you pick up the guitar. All these measures help protect your picking-hand fingernails, too, if you are using those.

As the skin toughens, some people find that their calluses get so thick that they actually catch on the strings and even break off. A little filing with an emery board can help smooth the calluses out, and if your fingertips get dry and cracked, soaking them in Vaseline or something similar (overnight, with a Band-Aid covering them) can be soothing. Just make sure they're not still greased up when you play again.

Will these painful ruts across my fingertips ever go away?

These kinds of difficulties are most easily straightened out in person, with a teacher looking at exactly how your fingers are falling on your guitar. But there are some common problems that beginners face, so here are a few ideas.

First, to diagnose your precise trouble spot, hold down the chord in question and play the strings one at a time, listening for which one is thumping rather than ringing out. Make sure that your finger is pressing the string down just behind the fret (toward the tuners), rather than directly over the fret or in the middle between two frets. Use just enough force to hold the string down firmly—don't mash it against the fingerboard.

Another likely cause of muted strings is that one of your other fingers is in the way. In the basic C fingering on the next page, for instance, it is very easy to inadvertently mute the fourth string by leaning your ring finger (which is playing the third fret of the fifth string) against it. If you straighten that finger up, the fourth string will

In some chord positions, my fingers don't "fit" right, or else I can't get all the strings to ring out. Any troubleshooting tips?

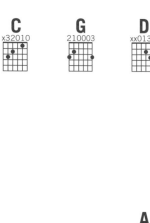

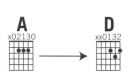

The ring finger in this D chord is falling too flat and muting the first string.

start ringing again. Same goes with the G chord: if the fourth string is muted, the finger holding the fifth string at the second fret is probably the culprit. And with a D, you might be silencing the first string by leaning your ring finger against it, as shown in the photo. (If you are not sure how to read these chord diagrams, see page 100.)

When beginners talk about their fingers not "fitting," chances are they are referring to the A chord—specifically the fingering at left with the index, middle, and ring fingers all in a row.

Some people's fingers are so thick (or the string spacing on the guitar is so narrow) that they just won't fit like this without pushing one of the fingers practically back to the first fret. In this situation, an alternate fingering might help, like the A position at left with the index tucked between your middle and ring fingers.

My thin fingers line up in a row without difficulty, but I prefer this fingering anyway because it gives me a nice pivot for going to the D chord—that is, my first finger can stay in place at the second fret of the third string for both chords.

There are also two- and one-finger options for the A that do the trick for some people. In the first version at left, your index finger takes care of two strings and your middle finger grabs one. In the second version, you lay your index finger down across all three strings. This position can come in very handy, but it requires more strength than the others, and some people's index finger joints just won't bend to get out of the way of the first string.

As you can see from these examples, there are various ways to finger chords, and different options will be more efficient in different situations or simply feel better for different fingers. Experienced guitarists know a few ways of grabbing a chord, which they can pull out of their bag of tricks as needed.

How can I train my fingers to go smoothly from one chord to another?

Practice. Practice. And did I mention practice?

Seriously, if there is one thing that guitar teachers agree on, it is that we learn most effectively by isolating a small problem, creating a simple exercise, and repeating and repeating and repeating it, as slowly as we need to, until we get it right. If you are having trouble going from a G chord to a C, slow it down and do that single change over and over until you think you are going to go out of your tree—and at that point you will have it.

Some other tips:

Visualize the chord shapes. "What slows people down is that they move one finger at a time instead of moving into the whole shape at once," says master teacher Bill Purse. "If you move the first finger, then the second, then the third, you are not going to get it." As a way to burn the whole chord shape in your memory, Carol McComb recommends holding the shape, scrambling your fingers, holding the shape, scrambling your fingers, etc., until your fingers spring into action the instant you see or think "D." The more your instincts take over, the less you have to look at your fingers, which always slows you down.

Aim for the bass string (the lowest note in the chord) first, because that is the one you hit first when you strum. When you are moving to a G, for instance, if you get your finger down on the third fret of the sixth string quickly, that will buy you some time to get your other fingers in place. Every split second helps.

Look for places where you can leave a finger in the same place during a chord change, or maybe slide it just one fret, rather than lifting all your fingers off the fingerboard and replanting them. For instance, if you play the A fingering at right, you can slide the third finger up a fret to play the D fingering at right. That'll keep you anchored during the move.

Finally, make sure you are keeping a steady tempo rather than pausing and then lurching ahead at the chord change. A metronome can help keep you honest; set the click as slow as you need to in order to play evenly and smoothly through the change, then speed up the tempo in small increments.

Is it best to focus on either rhythm or lead guitar, or to learn both?

In a band, lead guitarists seem to get the spotlight and the glory, while rhythm players chunka-chunk away in the background. Many beginners are, naturally enough, in a hurry to learn all those cool, gravity-defying lead licks, but the truth is that rhythm is the essential starting point for guitar. No band can function without a solid rhythm player; if the lead player is at home with the flu, the party goes on. As Jimmy Tomasello puts it, "The world is full of half-ass lead guitar players who can't play 12-bar rhythm in Bb. All the music comes from the chords and the harmony and keeping time. If you can't keep time, no one will want to hear what you have to say."

On the other hand, there is a lot to be said for early exposure to playing simple melodies and lead as you work on your rhythm basics. Many teachers point out that there is a big gender gap here—girls and women tend to stick with rhythm and never explore lead, while guys make that leap early and easily. "I find that especially women are much less intimidated if they learn notes and chords at the same time," says Marcy Marxer. "It doesn't matter if they are not aiming for, say, flatpicking or jazz [lead styles]. It just helps people have an overall concept of the guitar, and it sounds good." Marxer has ways of introducing lead to even rank beginners: they learn a couple of chords, and then she shows them how they can jam over those chords using just one note, by varying the rhythm. This may not be fancy but it is real improvisation, and it helps to demystify the world of lead guitar.

Players who focus only on rhythm and accompaniment often orient themselves on the guitar entirely with visual chord shapes—clusters of fingers on frets. Learning to play simple melodies and lead lines opens the door to understanding the individual notes on the fingerboard; even if you continue to focus on accompaniment, knowledge of the notes directly feeds into new chords and new sounds. The more skills you have, the more options and possibilities will open up on your guitar.

How can I get barre chords to ring out clearly?

As you ask the question, thousands of other beginners are nodding their heads emphatically, thinking, "Yeah, how do you do that?" **Barre chords**—those chord positions in which one of your fingers (usually the index) lies flat across several or all of the strings and heroically presses them down—have the reputation of being the single biggest hurdle that you have to clear in learning to play, and veteran players often remember their first clean F barre chord as a historic victory. But the truth is, players learn to tackle the dreaded barre chord every day, and contrary to popular belief, they don't all have Olympian finger muscles. You need some finger strength, it's true, but what you need even more is good technique—hands and arms placed correctly and energy used efficiently.

A series of building blocks prepares you for understanding barre chords and playing them clearly, which is why most guitar teachers introduce them well into the lesson plan. "There's a time for it," says Bill Purse. "You'll know when you're ready. You've got to get a whole series of chords in first position under your belt first. At that point you will have built up enough strength in the fingers." He also drills students on the notes on the fifth and sixth strings, which are the **root notes** of the basic barre chord forms and therefore tell you the name of the chord you're playing.

Cathy Fink uses the analogy of the capo to help players understand what's going on in a barre chord. "After people know their E chord or their A minor or their A chords, and they understand the use of the capo—how moving the capo up and down the neck changes what chords they're playing or what key they're playing in—then we can demonstrate barre chords and how they work pretty simply."

For instance, play an E chord with the alternate fingering at left, using your middle, ring, and pinky fingers. Your index finger becomes available to take on the role of the capo. You can move the E chord up a fret, with your first finger barring the whole first fret.

And then you can keep moving that up, just as you might move the capo into different positions on the neck. "I think once people use their imagination that the

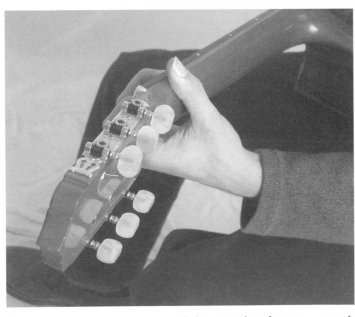 

To play a clean barre chord, don't let your thumb creep around toward the fingerboard. Keep it behind the neck, as in the right photo.

finger is like a fake capo," says Fink, "it just snaps right into place how barre chords really work."

How about getting rid of that depressing thunk you get when you try a barre chord? Well, here are some troubleshooting tips:

- As with any chord, make sure you are pressing down the string right next to the fret—you always get a cleaner sound this way.

- Make sure all the strings are being pressed down by the fleshy parts of your barre finger, not stuck in a groove at the joint. A slight move up or down can get the string out of this little rut in your finger, which is bound to mute it.

- Don't overextend your first finger above the neck (it shouldn't poke above the fingerboard).

- Don't press too hard. Concentrate instead on finger position.

- Try adjusting your left arm's position; instead of tucking your elbow in by your side, rotate it out slightly to gain a bit more leverage.

- Remember that in a typical barre chord, your barre finger is only pressing down a few of the strings, so focus your efforts on those strings and don't worry about the others.

- Make sure your thumb is well behind the neck. "If it creeps around at all, you can't put your index finger across in a straight line," says Carol McComb. "The further around your thumb reaches, the more you are inclined to bend your index finger." And use your thumb to support the effort of your finger.

- And finally, as with learning any new skill, take it slowly, starting with just a few minutes at a time. You can also ease into the full six-string barre chord by playing partial barre chords first—for instance, this four-string G fingering followed by the five-string one and finally the six-string version.

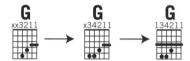

A little bit of practice, increasing gradually over successive days/week/months, will get you there eventually.

Any tips for learning to sing and play at the same time?

Singing and playing simultaneously can seem, at first, a little like rubbing your belly and tapping your head at the same time. You need to coordinate your two hands to keep a steady rhythm on the guitar and then keep track of the melody, which moves at a different pace. On top of all that, you're trying to keep your voice on pitch and remember the words!

So how do you teach yourself to do this kind of multitasking? By simplifying and practicing the individual components, then putting them all together. First of all, choose a song that is comfortable to sing, has familiar words, and uses a small number of simple chords that don't change too frequently. Save that favorite song with the tricky chord positions and fast changes for later. In magazines and books and on the Web, you'll find arrangements of pop songs with simplified chords and accompaniment parts, which might work well for this purpose. Simply choosing an accessible song might be enough to get you up and running, but if not, read on.

Mark Dvorak recommends building the song literally from the ground up. "A good approach is to chant the words," he says. "That is, put the syllables where you think they belong while you strum or pick your guitar arrangement. Slower is better, as it gives you time to hear what's supposed to happen.

"If it's still difficult, try simplifying the accompaniment. If you work your way through the progression strumming only the first beat of each measure, you'll be reducing the job to some pretty basic terms. You can also try chanting and strumming with a friend or a small group. Try it together, or experiment with one person only chanting and not strumming. Have someone else only strum and not chant. The others will have strong models of each as they try to do both."

From there, you can add in elements one at a time—the melody, a steady strum, then a more elaborate accompaniment part. Soon you will be ready to serenade your family, your friends, your dog, or just the four walls of your room.

The Learning Process

As mentioned elsewhere in these pages, you should approach practicing by taking small, well-planned steps. "Just like everything else in your life that you've learned, from the alphabet on, repetition is how you learn," says Cathy Fink. "You have to get comfortable with the concept that you are going to play the same thing 400 times before it comes to you without thinking, and once it comes to you without thinking, you're ready to move on to the next thing.

"What I like to do is to break things down into small steps and say, OK, the first thing you're going to do is practice this technique with your right hand—do that for about five minutes or until it's comfortable. If you start getting hand cramps, stretch out, take a break, shake your fingers around, and come back to it. And then when that feels comfortable, practice your right hand with this one chord under your left hand. Just practice taking off your hand and putting it back on that chord. Breaking things down into those small bits and doing them in the correct sequence really helps people make progress."

The other key to success is practicing regularly—make time every day or close to it, even if you can spare only 20 minutes. "People who practice only once or twice a week will never get any better," says Old Town School of Folk Music guitar teacher Jacob Sweet. "They will only stay in the same spot or regress. It is amazing to me how many of my adult students don't realize this." Short, frequent sessions can be very effective—in fact, 20 minutes of focused practice will pay off more than an hour of distracted, aimless playing.

The way you structure an individual practice session also makes a difference. Give yourself a few minutes to warm up and get in the groove by playing something you can do well and enjoy, rather than diving right into the hard stuff. But don't just coast through the entire session.

You may find a few tools to be useful. Bill Purse finds that practice journals help some people focus on specific goals. "Write yourself a little list," he says. "Where do I want to be with the guitar in six months? Where do I want to be in a year? And then work back from that." Other practice tools include a metronome, for keeping a steady beat as well as disciplining yourself to slow things down and then bring them gradually up to tempo; and a tape or digital recorder, for preserving your lessons and getting honest feedback on what you sound like. If you are working out of books, a music stand makes life much easier—it improves your playing position (no more hunching over the table) as well as your sightlines.

What's the most effective way to practice?

Of course, in this hyper-scheduled age, finding the *time* to play is the greatest challenge for most people—especially adults but increasingly kids as well. As with exercising or brushing your teeth, you need to have a regular time and place for the guitar in order to make it part of your daily life. Find a quiet spot where you won't be interrupted by family members or phone calls, and when the allotted time comes, just go do it before you have a chance to think about all the other stuff you really *should* be doing. If you don't clear the time and defend it, something else will fill the space—this is a law of physics of contemporary life.

If you have a guitar teacher, talk with him or her openly about these time issues—it will be frustrating to both of you if your practicing is not keeping pace with your lessons. Once you agree on a time commitment, your teacher can help you create an effective and realistic practice routine that's cued to the material you're covering in class. A good teacher will be able to map out the sequential steps of learning, rather than throw a whole bunch of new things at you at once, leaving you unsure of where to start.

Many of these things will fall into place very naturally if you just have good music to practice in the first place—songs you really love, coming alive on your guitar note by note. When the excitement is there, the time miraculously becomes available, the goals become clear, and practicing doesn't really feel like practicing at all—it's just *playing*. A period when practicing becomes a real drudge may be an indication that you need to seek out some new inspiration, whether it be a different teacher, an in-store clinic, a jam partner, a good lesson book, or just a CD that lights up your ears and your imagination.

What are the advantages of learning with a teacher or teaching myself with a method book?

There is a lot to be said for having at least a few lessons with a teacher at the outset. Fundamental things like good body and hand position are much easier to explain and demonstrate in person, and you don't want to develop bad habits that are hard to break later on. The words in the method book and the notes on the accompanying CD will always be the same, while a good teacher customizes the lessons and repertoire for you. "People make sense of things relating to the guitar in their own special and sometimes convoluted ways," says Jacob Sweet, "and a teacher can adapt the presentation according to that. I have seen no books that are able to do this." You can jam with your teacher, and it can be exciting and illuminating to be that close to a skilled player. With many teachers, you can bring in a favorite song and have it roughly transcribed for you on the spot. If you are in a group rather than a private class, you may get less individual attention, but your fellow beginners are a tremendous resource for support and sharing.

Now how about the strengths of a good method book? It is logically laid out, step by step. Everything is presented for you in a nice, neat package, which you can work through at your own pace and come back to as often as you like, even months or years later. By comparison, your scribbled notes from class and your teacher's occasional handouts might not provide very good documentation of what you are learning. Plus, you can loop the same track on an instructional CD 50 times if you want to, while it would drive any teacher bonkers to demonstrate something for you that many times.

Your choice doesn't have to boil down to either a teacher or a book/CD, of course. Some teachers have developed very coherent handouts that give you all the material for easy reference. Some use published methods as well, which can give you the best of both approaches—your teacher can augment the "Red River Valley" type of repertoire in traditional methods with contemporary songs, for instance. And you can record your lessons; a digital recorder is a vast improvement over the cassette for this purpose, as it gives you clean audio that you can edit and then access as quickly as a CD track.

The type of teacher or method that might (or might not) work for you is a very individual matter. Most people wind up trying a variety of approaches over their playing lives—they might start off with a teacher, work with lesson books or songbooks for a while, then go for a period with no formal instruction at all, then sign up for a few workshops when progress seems to be coming to a halt. . . . Your needs will change over time, as will your options, depending on factors like free time, budget, location, and transportation (got wheels?).

Some teachers rely heavily on published music, while others use their own handouts or no written notation at all.

What factors should I consider in choosing a teacher?

The place to begin any search for a teacher is with yourself: the better you understand what and who it is you are looking for, the better equipped you will be to make the right choice. What styles of music interest you? What are your goals—to accompany yourself, sing with your family, play instrumental music, join a band, follow along at a jam session? What kind of commitment of time and energy are you ready to make to the guitar? As a beginner, you might not have the answers to all these questions—you might have a burning desire to play but not be sure exactly what you want to play. That's fine—the answer will emerge over time.

Guitar teachers come to this trade from all sorts of angles and with all sorts of philosophies. Outside of genres like classical guitar, there is nothing even close to a standardized approach, and many teachers have no formal training—they have developed their lesson plans on the fly. Teaching provides one of the few sources of steady income for full-time musicians, so the people giving lessons down at your local shop may be doing so more out of gotta-pay-the-bills necessity than a particular calling to be a teacher. That's fine, as long as they don't feel bitter about not being rock stars. They should relate well to students, be patient and enthusiastic, and have a clear, well-organized approach. And if they are going to teach you as a beginner, they should like working with beginners.

Although it might be tempting to study with the local guitar hero, remember that the best performer may not be the best teacher, and the greatest teacher may not be the greatest performer. Pay more attention to expertise in the classroom than onstage.

Here are some other issues to consider and discuss with prospective teachers. You should be able to locate candidates through music schools, college music departments, and guitar stores and by talking to local players—word usually spreads quickly about good teachers.

Chemistry and communication. Simply put, you have to feel comfortable with your teacher, whether playing, talking, or asking questions—especially questions you think are dumb or overly obvious.

Group vs. private. There are advantages both ways. In a private lesson, obviously the focus is on you and your individual progress. You can ask lots of questions and make specific requests. Your teacher can troubleshoot your technique very

Where to Find a Teacher

You should be able to locate teachers through local music schools, college music departments, guitar stores, recording studios, folk societies and other local music organizations, and players. Although there are a lot of guitar lessons online, the Internet isn't quite as helpful in finding actual teachers. Craigslist or local news sites may be helpful, and the following websites also list teachers, though they are not comprehensive: MusicStaff.com, the Music Teachers List (teachlist.com), Mel Bay's Teacher Registry (melbay.com/findateacher. asp), WholeNote Guitar Teacher Database (wholenote.com/teachers/ default.asp), Flatpicking Guitar Network (flatpick.ning.com/notes/ Instructors).

effectively. All these things will be harder in a group situation, but on the other hand a group class puts you in touch with others to share tips, commiserate about sore fingers, and maybe even find a picking pal.

"So much of learning an instrument is an isolated process," says Jimmy Tomasello. "It makes all the difference in the world to share and play with others. You learn so much by watching, too. It's like if you want to learn French, you can sit at home with the tapes and books and that's cool; however, get your butt to Paris or Quebec for a week and you're warp-speeding. I always recommend that beginners learn in a group because it's fun to share that initial awkwardness with others instead of one-on-one with a teacher, which could be intimidating to some folks."

Specialties. Find out about any specialties, in style or approach, a teacher has. If the specialties don't match up with your goals, can he or she deliver what it is you are looking for? It's unrealistic, for example, to expect a folkie guitarist to be able to teach you how to shred along with your favorite hard-rock CDs. As a beginner, you may be better off with a teacher who can expose you to a variety of styles that you can choose to pursue later on.

Written music. Some teachers use none, some a little, some a lot. And the notation that they use might be chord diagrams, tablature, standard notation, or some combination of these (see the music notation question on the next page). It's worth asking what they use and why; the answer will clue you into whether their general approach is more by ear or more formal.

Finances. Obviously, you need to know what the lessons cost and whether you can afford them for the longer term. Also find out about policies for scheduling and cancellation. Being a private guitar teacher can be a tough business, so respect your teacher's need for steady and reliable payments from students.

Time commitment. As mentioned above, you should be sure that you will be able to put in the practice time that your teacher expects. You'll find some teachers willing to work with you very casually, others who require a high level of commitment and intensity.

Teachers should be patient and understanding and have a clear, well-organized approach.

You can do an initial screening of teachers in a conversation, but once you have narrowed down to a likely candidate, take a trial lesson and see how it goes. A good teacher, says Bill Purse, "is kind of a coach and a cheerleader all in one." The playing is ultimately up to you, but there's nothing like having expertise and support on the sidelines.

T his is one of those hot-button issues endlessly debated by musicians and teachers. It's actually a more complex question than just "to read or not to read," because guitarists use and swear by several mongrel forms of notation, rather than one standard. As a group, guitarists have a well-deserved rap as bad music readers compared to other instrumentalists, as jazz musicians in particular love to point out. (Sample jab: How do you stop a guitarist from playing? Give him something to read.) But this doesn't change the fact that there is no direct correlation between being a great reader and being a great musician. Music notation is an extremely useful tool but not an end in itself.

Let's sort through this tangle by looking at the pros and cons of the basic types of guitar notation.

Should I learn to read standard notation or tablature?

Chord grids

Chord grids (also known as **chord diagrams** or **chord frames**) are the simplest form of guitar-specific notation, understandable to beginners in a matter of minutes. Take a look at these examples.

These are visual representations of the guitar fingerboard: The six strings are shown as vertical lines, with the sixth (lowest-pitched) string on the left and the first (highest-pitched) on the right. The dots show where you press down the string, and the numbers up top tell you which finger to use: 1 for the index, 2 for the middle, 3 the ring, 4 the pinky, and sometimes *T* for the thumb. *X* indicates a string that is muted or not played; 0 is an open string. The nut (which guides the strings at the tuner end of the fingerboard) is the thick horizontal line at the top. When the chord is played farther up the neck (toward the soundhole), a number to the right of the diagram shows you the **position** (fret).

Closely related to these graphic diagrams is the sort of text-only chord notation you'll see on the Internet, in which the numbers represent the frets and you are left on your own to figure out which finger to put where. For example, an E chord is 022100: open sixth string, second fret on the fifth string, second fret on the fourth string, first fret on the third string, top two strings open. An open D chord would be written XX0232.

The advantages of chord grids? They are clear, visual, and intuitive—very good for showing the basic chords of an accompaniment part. The main disadvantage is that they really work only for chord positions; they can't show you melodies or even little chord riffs. And they also tell you nothing about what notes you are playing, only the location of your fingers.

Tablature

Tablature (aka tab) is a very old form of notation that has come back with a vengeance and become the dominant way that nonclassical guitarists read music. Also graphically based, tab shows the six strings of the guitar as horizontal lines, with the first string on top and the sixth on the bottom. The numbers indicate which fret you play on a given string.

In tab, these lines are divided into measures, as with standard notation, but usually this is the only indication of rhythm that you get—mostly you just follow a sequence of fret positions and have to

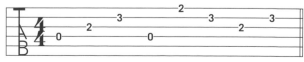

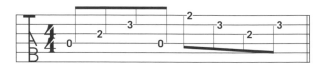

figure out the rhythm by listening to a recording. Sometimes you will encounter tab that includes rhythmic notation, as in the example at top left.

But even here, you are not being shown how long notes ring out—only when they start. This is why tab is commonly used in conjunction with standard notation (bottom left), which provides the missing information.

"Tab is easy to learn and very specific in the location of notes," says Frederick Noad. "Its weakness is that it does not express time values and sustained parts nearly as well as standard notation. It is worth learning anyway, since it was the original notation for guitar and lute and can be mastered in an hour or two."

Like chord diagrams, tablature shows you where to put your fingers but not what the music should sound like. This makes it a quick but limited way into learning a piece of music. You can play the same notes at several locations on the guitar, so ultimately it's best to see beyond the fret numbers in tablature and be able to hear the notes and perhaps come up with your own interpretation.

Tablature works better for fingerstyle guitar music or flatpicked solos, with their individually articulated notes, than for strumming. Most people also find it indispensable for alternate tunings; when the pitches of open strings are changed, trying to figure out a piece from standard notation only can cause cerebral meltdown.

Standard notation

Standard notation is what works for most other instruments—it tells you the pitch, rhythm, and duration of notes all in one compact package. Guitar music written this way often includes fingering information: little numbers next to noteheads tell you which fretting finger to use, and letters tell you which picking finger to use: *p* for thumb, *i* for index, *m* for middle, *a* for ring, *c* for pinky. Circled numbers indicate on which string to play a note, and often other interpretive guidance is given as well.

Among guitarists, you will most often find standard notation readers in the classical realm. Although "classics in tab" editions have become more common, the bulk of the repertoire is written only in standard notation. For classical players, says Ben Harbert, "in the long run, reading music is essential. Understanding phrasing, reading dynamics, having flexibility in fingerings, and transposing music from other instruments are all important parts of being a classical guitarist. I believe that students who have some experience with the guitar can begin with tab; otherwise, learning to read music can slow a student enough to be frustrated with the style. But the students I begin on tab inevitably want to learn to read music after they see the limitations of tab. And students with no experience can learn to read music at the level of their technical progress on the guitar."

The main advantage of standard notation, as alluded to above, is that it represents the actual sound of the notes rather than simply where you put your fingers, so it encourages you to listen more closely and make your own interpretation. It shows you the contour of a melody very clearly and includes a lot of detail about the feel, dynamics, and other nuances of the music. As for disadvantages, the primary one is that standard notation is simply harder to learn than tab or chord diagrams—although not nearly as hard as most guitarists think. It is more suited to solo instrumentals than to simple accompaniments, which are very efficiently shown with chord diagrams or tab, and it is inadequate for alternate-tunings styles.

No notation

From blues to flamenco, plenty of genres have flourished without a written note in sight. In the case of flamenco, as Frederick Noad points out, "a good ear and skill at memorizing are of the first importance. In Spain there was a time when guitarists who could read music were excluded from the flamenco fraternity." With the boom of instructional publishing, just about every style—including flamenco—is available transcribed and notated these days, but you can still make a lifetime of music without cracking open a single piece of sheet music.

In the end, keep in mind that music notation of whatever form is just shorthand. It allows someone else to communicate a piece of music to you on paper, or for you to jot down an idea for safekeeping or to share with other musicians. The further you go as a player, the more likely it is that you will want or need to do these things. There are limitations to what you can do as a musician—especially as a professional musician—without learning the written language.

But no matter what sort of notation you wind up using or not using, the essential thing is to be able to hear the music coming out of your guitar, rather than remain focused on fret numbers or chord shapes or eighth notes or anything else on the page.

Like all things digital, computer-based guitar instruction is evolving at a dizzying pace. The state-of-the-art programs as I began writing this answer will probably be obsolete by the end of the last paragraph, so I won't even try to pin down precisely what you can do with your guitar and your PC or Mac.

The potential is tremendous, though. Websites, CDs, DVDs, and the like can deliver a dazzling combination of audio, video, music notation, text, and interactive features that no other medium can match. You can click your way to the exact video view you want, watch the lyrics and tab scroll by, and slow down the music while maintaining the same pitch. You can plug in your guitar and see onscreen how well you are following along, or jam along with a virtual backup band. Software will help you look up a zillion chords in whatever tuning you like, zip through an encyclopedia of scales and modes, or simply tune your guitar.

The gee-whiz factor with computer instruction is very high; the challenge, as always, is for developers to bring solid teaching approaches to bear on the latest and hottest technology. Especially as a beginner, what you need is not unlimited options or techno razzle-dazzle but a smartly sequenced, clearly presented progression of lessons.

The pace of change in the computer world is both its greatest strength and its greatest weakness. You know how quickly that cutting-edge computer/software/peripheral winds up in a dusty box in your basement. Computer-based instruction on a fixed medium can be expected to have a similarly short shelf life—it's entirely possible that eventually you won't even be able to open that disc on

What kind of guitar instruction is available on the computer? How does this medium compare with books and videos?

Multimedia guitar instruction is proliferating all over the Web.

your PC, because the engine that runs it has disappeared from the market, and you had to replace the machine that did run it with something that keeps pace with the industry's latest offerings. And even if the disc still runs, it will quickly seem extremely primitive and limited compared to what's come out since. So don't expect any program to be useful as long as more stable media like books or even CDs and videos will be. But if you get a lot of value from it in the short term, great—grab your guitar and your mouse and have a blast.

These days, the Web and a high-speed connection to it are your best ticket to checking out what's available in multimedia guitar instruction. Free lessons, freeware, and shareware abound, and there are massive libraries of song lyrics and guitar tab. It's easy to find fellow computer/guitar heads who can recommend programs and sites as well as offer playing tips. Over time, expect to see more and more personalized instruction available on the Web, private as well as small group lessons with students scattered all over the globe. Where all this technology is going is never clear, but this much is definitely true: your computer can open up new horizons for you as a guitarist.

Are there any secrets to figuring out songs by ear?

The more you play and the more you listen, the sharper you will be at recognizing patterns and chord shapes in songs that you hear. After a while, the distinctive sound of an open G chord becomes ingrained in your memory, and when you hear a guitarist kicking off a song with that chord, you'll know it—bingo. The same holds true for all sorts of chords and licks: they eventually become part of a vocabulary of sounds that you recognize without even thinking.

There are some tips and tools that can help you along the way. Before you can get anywhere in figuring out a song, you need to be sure that you are in tune with the record. This is often a simple matter of tuning your guitar with an electronic tuner, but that doesn't work if the record isn't exactly at normal pitch—especially with older recordings, you may have to tweak your tuning slightly up or down.

The first thing to do is listen for what's called the **tonic**: the root note of the key that the song is in. For a song in the key of G, the tonic is a G note; in the key of C, it's a C; and so on. The tonic is the harmonic center of the song—the chords may travel away from that note, but eventually they come back and resolve on it. To find this note, first try your open sixth (E), fifth (A), fourth (D), and third (G) strings and see if any of them match the song you are trying to work out—E, A, D, and G are all very common keys for guitar songs. If those don't fit, play notes up and down the sixth string while listening to the track; you will feel it when you arrive at that critical note. If the note you are playing sounds very close to, but not precisely on, the tonic, and moving up or down a fret takes you further away, that's a clue that you may need to retune slightly.

Once you've got that note, you need to know what sort of chord sits on it. Let's say the tonic is a D—is it a bright-sounding D major or a darker, moodier D minor? Your ears will learn to tell the difference. Try out this process first on simple folk, country, or rock songs with just a few chords, and the tonic chord will almost always be a simple major or minor chord.

From here, learning a little bit about the chords typically found in each key is extremely helpful. I won't get into full-on description of chord theory here, but suffice it to say that a little dab of chord theory goes a long way in picking up music by ear. Here is a chart that shows the basic chords in the most common guitar keys (for simplicity's sake, I have left out some of the more complicated and less common chords). The Roman numerals in the top row indicate which degree of the scale the chord is built on (uppercase Roman numerals are used for major chords, and lowercase for minor). The I is the tonic chord, which tells you what key you're in (e.g., G is the I chord in the key of G; G is the first note of the scale in that key). The next most common chords are the IV and V (built on the fourth and fifth notes in the scale), and the other chords in the same row are likely suspects too. So if you have found that the song is in the key of A, for instance, look across the A row for other chords that are likely to crop up in your song, especially the IV (D) and V (E).

Major Keys

I	ii	iii	IV	V or V7	vi
C	Dm	Em	F	G or G7	Am
D	Em	F#m	G	A or A7	Bm
E	F#m	G#m	A	B or B7	C#m
G	Am	Bm	C	D or D7	Em
A	Bm	C#m	D	E or E7	F#m

Minor Keys

i	III	iv	v or V7	VI	VII or VII7
Am	C	Dm	Em or E7	F	G or G7
Em	G	Am	Bm or B7	C	D or D7
Dm	F	Gm	Am or A7	B♭	C or C7

Also very useful is some understanding of common **chord progressions**: sequences of chords that crop up again and again in songs. If you know, for instance, that the V chord usually resolves to the I chord, you have a significant clue to where the chord progression might go in your song. You know this intuitively—when you're playing or listening to something in the key of C, for instance, you feel the tug from a G chord (the V) back toward C (the I). But knowing this fact intellectually as well as intuitively is another arrow in your quiver.

In addition to using this kind of information to help you find the chords, you can apply the method mentioned above of searching for the root of a particular chord by trying open strings or moving around the sixth string. Once you know the root, it's pretty easy to zero in on the exact chord.

As you spin the song, listen closely for open strings, which have a bright ring that's distinctly different from fretted notes. Most guitarists use chords with a lot of open strings—call it laziness, or call it just being smart. This brings up one very important rule for learning songs off records: the correct answer is most likely the easiest one. If you find yourself having to tie your fingers into knots to play along, you are probably missing some essential piece of information.

Like the presence of a capo. Let's say you've discovered that a song by your favorite songwriter/guitarist is in the knuckle-busting key of E♭. But you could swear that you hear something that sounds like a D chord, with maybe an A and G thrown in there too. What's going on here? Most likely, a capo at the first fret, which raises those D, A, and G fingerings so that you hear them as E♭, B♭, and A♭.

A bigger monkey wrench is thrown in when the song is not played in standard tuning—you will hear open strings ringing that are simply not available on your guitar. Identifying alternate tunings by ear can be tough, which is why many people rely on transcriptions in magazines and songbooks and on the Web to supply the critical information about how the guitar is tuned. Artist sites often include lists of tunings that are invaluable. If the tuning or transcription was posted by a fan on an "unofficial" site, it may or may not be correct, but even checking out an inaccurate version may give you ideas about how to do it right. And coming up with your own rendition, in a different tuning or even in standard tuning, is just as valid as re-creating the original. Even if the song is not in a weird tuning, these in-print or online transcriptions are a great resource.

In the heyday of the LP, lots of musicians learned songs by slowing the album down to half speed, which was a great trick but had the unfortunate side effect of lowering all the notes by an octave. These days there are stand-alone boxes and software that do the same thing without changing the pitch—very handy "hearing aids" used by professional transcribers all the time.

So there are plenty of tools potentially at your disposal, but remember that going through this process with nothing but your ears and your fingers is educational way beyond figuring out how to play a specific song. You learn a tremendous amount by trying to pin down how to re-create sounds without following a written recipe. Even if you get it wrong, through trial and error you discover a lot about how songs and guitars work.

What are alternate tunings, and why do so many guitarists use them?

Alternate tunings are simply what you get when you twiddle the notes of your open strings away from the pitches E A D G B E (from the lowest-pitched string to the highest), also known as standard tuning. This is not a new idea. Standard tuning came into being around the late 1700s, and the guitar family goes back a lot further than that. The concept of tuning the strings to a chord (often called an **open tuning**) is basic to blues and other traditions. Modern guitarists may feel that they are on the cutting edge by using different tunings for different songs, but they are simply the latest in a long line of stringed-instrument players to do this.

The simplest alternate tuning, and the one that just about everybody uses, is known as **dropped D**: lowering the sixth string to D. When you also drop the first string to D, you've got **double dropped D** (aka **D modal**), widely used by Neil Young and others. The most common open tunings are **open G** (D G D G B D, a G-major chord), **open D** (D A D F♯ A D, a D-major chord), and **open C** (C G C G C E, a C-major chord). Open G and open D are the staples of slide guitar and country blues. Also popular in Celtic music and other genres is the tuning referred to as **"dad gad"**: D A D G A D. From there, the variations are endless.

So why bother changing the tuning of your guitar and thereby hopelessly confusing your hard-earned knowledge of where notes are on the fingerboard? First, to make things easier by making certain notes available on open strings. If you are playing a song in the key of D, dropped-D tuning is very convenient because it gives you a nice low root note on the sixth string. If you are playing slide, having the open strings tuned to a chord means that you can play melodies and licks over the open strings—simultaneous lead and backup—and then play other big fat chords by moving your slide up the neck.

In an alternate tuning, you can also play complex chords with very little effort—a Dm7(add6) is actually accomplished with just two fingers once you are in double-dropped-D tuning. In fact, with an alternate tuning, you can play chord voicings that are unreachable in standard tuning. For songwriters and instrumentalists looking for new sounds, this is a major attraction—play impossible jazz chords without even trying! And the kicker is that you don't have to know what you're doing, theoretically speaking: if you are in an unfamiliar tuning, what you know about fingerings no longer applies, so you can freely hunt and peck and experiment. You can even play chords and licks you know in standard tuning and hear what bizarre sounds come out! Alternate-tunings junkies talk about this process in mystical tones—they love getting lost in an entirely new guitar landscape and discovering sounds they never would have found intentionally or consciously. As Joni Mitchell once put it, changing your tuning is like rearranging the letters on your keyboard and then typing away—you are sure to come up with some new words!

Sounds enticing, doesn't it? It is, but alternate tunings can also be very confusing, especially if you are just gaining your footing (fingering, I mean) on the guitar. So as a beginner, you should stick to one tuning until you've gained some experience. Standard tuning is plenty to keep anyone busy, and it has its own unique advantages, such as the flexibility to give you open-string roots in a variety of keys. It is good to realize, though, that a whole new universe of sounds becomes available by retuning your strings, and in many styles of contemporary music, alternate tunings are challenging the very "standardness" of standard tuning.

Sharing Your Music

How can I find people to jam with, and how should I prepare for those sessions?

Jam sessions come in all shapes and sizes, from siblings belting out pop hits to campfire song circles to house parties to sit-ins down at the jazz club or Irish pub. Although some of these confabs have an element of competitiveness, good jams are all about good times and companionship, and a beginner strumming along is as welcome as a professional guitar slinger.

It can be hard to find or start a jam session, but once one gets going, it is even harder to stop. Prime places to scout for jam sessions or playing partners have been mentioned elsewhere in these pages: guitar classes, music camps, festivals, music stores . . . A guitar shop might have a board where you can post a notice about your interests and ability level and who/what you are looking for. Local publications, especially free ones, sometimes have active "musicians' exchange" listings, and many websites also feature musician classifieds and referral services, although they cast a very wide geographical net. Open-mic nights draw players of all stripes and can be a great place for making connections, even if you are not taking the stage. In many communities there are small organizations of musicians and aficionados—for songwriters, folkies, blues mavens, etc. Poke and ask around; you might be surprised at what you find in your town.

When you do meet someone, it is a big help if you can concretely describe your interests. Make a short list of artists and records you love, and start collecting songs you play or want to play in a notebook: think especially about songs that others might know, are straightforward to pick or sing along with, and are more on the festive side than moody personal reflections. Jam sessions often have awkward moments when everyone is rifling through their internal song indexes to think of the next thing to play, and your songbook could really keep things moving. And if you can come up with that fourth verse that eludes everyone else's memory, you are a major asset to the group! Also, there are some great books available for finding lyrics and song ideas (one I find particularly useful is *Rise Up Singing*—see the Resources chapter).

Aside from your songbook, a capo is a very handy jam-session accessory in many situations. It allows you to change the key to suit people's voices or instruments better, without having to play different fingerings. If another guitarist puts a capo at the second fret and starts playing something, match that capo position and watch his or her

In a jam session, rhythm rules. Concentrate on nailing the chord changes and keeping a steady beat.

fingers—that'll make it much easier to join in.

Effective jam session preparations will vary depending on the style and setting, but there are a few universal truths. Most important, rhythm rules, so work hard on nailing the chord changes and keeping a steady beat. Simplify a part you are still trying to master down to something that you can do without thinking or pausing. Without solid rhythm, everything falls apart, whereas the frills can go away and not be missed at all. Also, train yourself to listen and be flexible with the arrangement of a song—you might need to let an intro chord sit there for a few extra measures, for instance, while the singer is trying to think of the next verse. When someone is singing or taking a lead, kick back and give them room to be heard. And finally, stick with a winning theme. If everyone is having a blast singing Beatles songs, try to come up with something in the same vein. If you don't know anything along those lines, do a little homework before your next gathering. Everyone will light up when you kick into one of their favorite songs—it's like discovering you have a close friend in common.

---

et's see . . . a quick flip through *Acoustic Guitar* magazine's annual guide to summer workshops reveals courses in acoustic blues and slide, chamber music for classical guitar and mandolin, six- and seven-string Brazilian guitar and cavaquinho, Cape Breton fiddle tunes, rock soloing, western swing, songwriting, alternate tunings, music theory, and Gypsy jazz—not to mention building and repairing guitars—in locations from Manhattan to Mallorca. You get the idea.

What kind of camps or workshops are there for guitarists?

Nowadays there are camps catering to all ages and styles, some following the traditional camp model of a rustic setting with camping or cabins, others taking place in comfortable hotels or at urban locations with day-only attendance. The vibe of these gatherings varies quite a bit, from nonstop revelry to more studious and structured atmospheres.

Many professional players enjoy taking a hiatus from the road and teaching at these camps, so you will find opportunities to study with people whose music you know and love. And, of course, your fellow campers are a big draw. Jamming tends to happen all over the place and at all hours, and at many camps the instructors help to organize and lead sessions. There are also usually open-mic venues for those who want a taste of the stage.

Most camps offer extensive beginner programs, and you can learn an awful lot in a week of living and breathing guitar music (don't forget to sleep at least a little). Beyond good old word-of-mouth, websites offer complete information about camps, so surf around for options that fit your personality, interests, and budget (see the Resources chapter for a few starting points). Find out about what sorts of beginner classes camps offer, and if guided slow jams and other beginner-oriented activities are part of the package.

Music camps and workshops (a National Guitar Workshop classroom is shown here) cater to all ages and musical styles.

If you feel that you are pursuing your music in isolation, or that every other guitarist in the world is much more skilled and savvy than you are, a camp is a surefire cure. You will see that everyone has to clear the same basic hurdles in learning an instrument and that music really takes flight when you gather with kindred spirits.

How can I get ready to step onstage for the first time?

You can gain valuable performing experience without going anywhere near a stage. Start right at your house: a parent, sibling, spouse, or close friend can make a great first audience for a set that could consist of only one song. You might be able to coax someone into singing or playing with you, which can make things more comfortable the first time out.

Further afield, look for playing opportunities at parties, barbecues, and other social gatherings. And if you are ready to put together an actual set list and do a little show, you can find extremely appreciative and thoroughly nonintimidating audiences at places like senior centers and schools.

When you are ready for a more formal performance situation, open-mic nights are a perfect place to get your feet wet on an actual stage with a real PA system, and they have the fringe benefit of introducing you to fellow musicians in the area. You usually are limited to a couple of songs, so no extensive repertoire is required, and relative beginners are often part of the lineup. Scores of solo artists and bands have gotten started this way. It might seem intimidating to play for an audience of primarily musicians, but they have been exactly in your shoes, and for the most part I have found them to be appreciative and supportive.

Then there are the casual settings where your audience may or may not pay any attention to you—cafés, restaurants, bookstores, receptions, office parties, the street . . . the bread-and-butter (or bagel-and-cream-cheese) gigs for many musicians. Is it depressing to play guitar for people while they clink their glasses and talk about the traffic and never notice that you just executed a particularly soulful rendition of a classic song? Sure, it can be. But it's also liberating. These sorts of gigs can be like a heightened form of practice, with only one time through each tune (except on the street, where you can play the same five songs all day if you want to) and the possibility of tip money. If a song does break through the chatter and get a reaction, that is a minor miracle and very gratifying.

A well-planned set list is a big advantage in performing. Your first song has to allow both you and your audience to get into the groove, so make it something you can play in a relaxed fashion, and save your tough stuff for later. Think about all the many types of contrasts from song to song, and incorporate changes of key, tempo, length, and mood. These are good both for your audience's ears and for you as a player to stay at the top of your game.

Your first song has to allow both you and your audience to get into the groove.

The best way to get ready for a performance of any type is to practice as realistically as you can. That means do a true dress rehearsal: Sit if you are going to sit, stand if you're going to stand, and start at the beginning and go right through to the end without restarting any songs or stopping for ten minutes of tuning and snacking. If you make a mistake, force yourself to plow ahead in the least awkward manner possible. Recovering from flubs is an essential performing skill, and you can practice it. Just keep the rhythm going and circle back around to the beginning of the line, or forget about your mistake and concentrate on nailing the rest of the song—your audience will forget about your momentary lapse, if they even noticed it in the first place.

It's an adrenaline rush to put yourself out there for an audience and feel the energy waves come back at you. You may get hooked and decide to dedicate yourself to doing this for a living. But remember that you can perform music for people without ever becoming a Performer. Don't let a lack of career aspirations stop you from experiencing the buzz of sharing your music. Playing guitar is much too important an activity to be left to the professionals.

There is a natural ebb and flow to learning—I don't think it's possible or even desirable to be blasting ahead all the time. You might pick up a whole bunch of new things really fast, then need to spend a period of time assimilating all that information and resting up for the next challenges.

We have so much instant gratification available to us these days, from pay-per-view cable to online shopping, that it is easy to become impatient with the pace of learning an instrument. No matter how hard you practice or how good your guitar is or how sophisticated the method you are using, it just takes time to advance. Not only are you developing calluses and training minute muscles in your fingers, but you are constantly refining your internal sense of harmony, melody, and rhythm. Actually practicing the guitar is only part of what helps us improve. The rest of the progress is in the expansion of our soul and imagination, and time spent away from the guitar can do as much to develop these intangible things as concentrated playing.

Still, everybody experiences that feeling of being in a rut, and the accompanying drain of enthusiasm for the guitar. There are many things that might help nudge you back on the road. Maybe you've gone as far as you can with your teacher, book, video, or whatever tool you are using, and some new instruction with a different approach might be just the ticket. If you have been in a group class, maybe some individual attention is what you need, or if you have been taking private lessons, maybe some group interaction would do wonders for you. As elaborated above, connecting with other musicians is a real energizer. Another player will always have somewhat different interests than you do, and trying to find common ground will suggest new projects or goals and give you a powerful incentive to achieve them.

Or you might need to simply open your ears a little wider. Everything we hear is ultimately the fuel for everything we play, and a new artist or style—especially experienced in person rather than on record—might suggest avenues for the guitar that you have never even considered or may simply rekindle the flame that started you on this playing quest in the first place.

It is easy to fall into the trap of blaming your guitar for a lack of progress, and some of the greatest guitar music of all time has been made on cheap instruments that any guitar snob would snort at. But it is possible to reach a point at which your guitar limits what you can do, and a new, better, or just plain different instrument can inspire a new wave of learning. Oftentimes you're not even really aware of the ways in which a particular guitar shapes the music you play on it. For a long time I played a small-bodied instrument that sounded very nice for solo fingerstyle music,

Sometimes I feel like my playing is in a rut, and I start to lose interest. What can I do to stay inspired?

which I hadn't explored much at all before. When I replaced it with a bigger instrument that had a much fuller sound and volume to burn, I suddenly rediscovered the raw power of rock rhythm and started playing all kinds of songs in that vein. So if you suspect your current guitar is holding you back somehow, you might try browsing in music stores or borrowing something different—but only do this if you are prepared to follow through on getting a new guitar. No sense in deepening your dissatisfaction with an instrument that you are going to be playing for the foreseeable future—and there is still plenty of undiscovered music in that guitar anyway.

For me, what sparks progress on the guitar is having some kind of project; arbitrarily selecting something (picking exercises or a song out of a book that contains certain technical challenges, for instance) never works—I lack that kind of discipline, I guess. The projects that really stick come organically out of listening, preparing for an upcoming gig or get-together, or exploring a new idea I happen upon. My guitar is never more alive for me than it is when I am writing a song—I will play something over and over till my fingers are killing me, trying to get my head and hands around it and understand where it is leading. The same thing holds true regardless of whether you write songs or "compose" in any formal sense: what drives learning are these moments when you can feel music being created right under your fingers.

Not a bad accomplishment for two hands, some pieces of wood, and six strings.

Resources

Instruction

Print

The guitar instruction field is teeming with products. Here are a few written by people interviewed for this book or mentioned specifically in the text. For a broad selection, browse a local music store or one of the catalogs listed under mail-order sources below.

Peter Blood-Patterson, ed., *Rise Up Singing,* Sing Out. Extremely useful compendium of lyrics and chord progressions for 1,200 songs. Strong folk orientation, but a good sampling of '60s and '70s pop/rock as well.

David Hamburger, *The Acoustic Guitar Method,* String Letter. A three-volume method from the publishers of *Acoustic Guitar* magazine (and this book), based on songs and techniques from American roots music, with supplemental songbooks. Also available: *The Acoustic Guitar Fingerstyle Method.*

Cathy Fink and Marcy Marxer, *Kids' Guitar Songbook,* Homespun. Individually and together, Fink and Marxer have a number of other good books and videos. For a complete list, see cathymarcy.com.

Carol McComb, *Country and Blues Guitar for the Musically Hopeless*, Klutz Press.

Frederick Noad, *Solo Guitar Playing,* Vols. 1 and 2, Schirmer; ***The Complete Idiot's Guide to Playing the Guitar***, Macmillan.

Jessica Baron Turner, *SmartStart Guitar,* Hal Leonard. A kids' guitar method, in book/CD or on video. Turner is also the author of *How to Raise a Musical Child*, from String Letter Publishing.

Online

Acoustic Guitar, AcousticGuitar.com

Berklee Music, berkleemusic.com

Break Down Way, breakdownway.com

Guitar Noise, guitarnoise.com

Guitar Player, guitarplayer.com

Harmony Central, harmony-central.com

JamPlay, jamplay.com

True Fire, truefire.com

WholeNote, wholenote.com

WorkshopLive, workshoplive.com

Instruments

Acoustic Guitar Owner's Manual, String Letter Publishing.

Tony Bacon, *Electric Guitars: The Illustrated Encyclopedia,* Thunder Bay.

Dan Erlewine, *Guitar Player Repair Guide: How to Set Up, Maintain, and Repair Electrics and Acoustics,* Backbeat Books.

Frets.com. Frank Ford's exhaustive, authoritative site on acoustic guitar care and repair.

Mail-Order Sources

Elderly Instruments
PO Box 14249
Lansing, MI 48901
(888) 473-5810
(517) 372-7890
Fax (517) 372-5155
elderly.com
Comprehensive catalog of guitar books and products, with useful descriptions.

JK Lutherie
11115 Sand Run
Harrison, OH 45030
Orders (800) 344-8880
(513) 353-3320
jklutherie.com
Specializes in instrument books.

Music Dispatch
(800) 637-2852
musicdispatch.com
Mail-order for Hal Leonard Publishing and its many distributed lines.

Sheetmusicdirect.com
Downloadable sheet music.

Sheetmusicplus.com
1300 64th St.
Emeryville, CA 94608
(800) 743-3868
(512) 420-7121
Extensive catalog from many publishers.

String Letter Publishing
PO Box 767
San Anselmo, CA 94979-0767
(415) 485-6946
Fax (415) 485-0831
StringLetter.com
The publisher of this book offers a variety of guitar instruction and reference works, including The *Acoustic Guitar Method*, with free sample lessons on the website.

Music Camps

The following is a small sampling of organizations that run workshops and camps. For an extensive, searchable list, with links and specialties (updated annually), visit AcousticGuitar.com.

Augusta Heritage Center
Davis and Elkins College
100 Campus Dr.
Elkins, WV 26241
(304) 637-1209
Fax (304) 637-1317
augustaheritage.com

Berklee College of Music
1140 Boylston St
Boston, MA 02215
(617) 266-1400
Fax (617) 747-2047
berklee.edu

Centrum
PO Box 1158
Port Townsend, WA 98368
(360) 385-3102
Fax (360) 385-2470
centrum.org

National Guitar Workshop
PO Box 222
Lakeside, CT 06758
(800) 234-6479
Fax (860) 567-0374
guitarworkshop.com

Steve Kaufman's Acoustic Kamp
PO Box 1020
Alcoa TN 37701
(800) FLATPIK
acoustic-kamp.com

The Swannanoa Gathering
Warren Wilson College
PO Box 9000
Asheville, NC 28815-9000
(828) 298-3434
swangathering.org

Index of Guitar Lingo

Page numbers indicate where a term is most fully explained and illustrated.

About the Authors

Jason Garoian

Acoustic Guitar's production coordinator Jason Garoian spends his days advancing the magazine's offerings on the Web, and in his spare time writes songs, sings, and plays guitar for San Francisco blues/noise trio the Discontinued Models (myspace. com/thediscontinuedmodels). He considers learning to play guitar to be one of the best decisions he's ever made.

David Hodge

David Hodge has for years provided backup to numerous Berkshire County, Massachusetts, singer-songwriters. But teaching music is his first love; in addition to his private students, he teaches group guitar lessons for the Berkshire Community College. And guitar students of all ages and levels from more than 168 countries read his lessons at Guitar Noise (guitarnoise.com). He is the author of *The Complete Idiot's Guide to Playing Bass Guitar* (Alpha Books).

Adam Levy

As a longstanding member of Norah Jones' Handsome Band, Adam Levy's electric and acoustic guitar work can be heard in cafés worldwide. Of his own jazz-tinged recordings, the release *Loose Rhymes—Live on Ludlow Street* (Lost Wax, lostwaxmusic.com) marks his debut as a performing songwriter. Levy's instructional book and DVD *Play the Right Stuff: Creating Great Guitar Parts* is available from Alfred Publishing (alfred.com). For more information, visit adamlevy.com.

Pete Madsen

Pete Madsen (buzzyfrets.com) is a guitarist, writer, and teacher living in the San Francisco Bay Area. He specializes in acoustic blues, ragtime, and slide guitar and has studied with the likes of Duck Baker and Joe Satriani. His latest CD, *Carnival of Rags*, is as much a tribute to the playing of Blind Blake, Merle Travis, Doc Watson, and Big Bill Broonzy as it is an expression of his own personal take on traditional fingerstyle guitar.

Adam Perlmutter

Adam Perlmutter (adamperlmutter.com) is a guitarist, transcriber, and writer living in New York City. He received a master's degree in contemporary improvisation from the New England Conservatory of music. He is a former music editor of *Guitar One* and *Guitar World Acoustic* magazines and is a regular contributor to *Acoustic Guitar*. His most recent instructional books are *Broadway Piano Songs for Dummies* and *Jim Hall— Signature Licks*, and his transcriptions have appeared in songbooks for all the leading music publishers, including Alfred, Cherry Lane, and Hal Leonard.

Jeffrey Pepper Rodgers

Jeffrey Pepper Rodgers (jeffreypepperrodgers.com) is the founding editor of *Acoustic Guitar* magazine and author of *Rock Troubadours* (a collection of conversations with Paul Simon, Jerry Garcia, Joni Mitchell, and more) and *The Complete Singer-Songwriter: A Troubadour's Guide to Writing, Performing, Recording, and Business*. Rodgers' song "Fly," from his solo CD *Humming My Way Back Home*, won a 2008 Lennon Award—and a grand prize—in the John Lennon Songwriting Contest. He lives outside Syracuse, New York, where he writes and edits for *Acoustic Guitar*, reports on the music scene for NPR's *All Things Considered*, and hosts the Words and Music Songwriter Showcase.

Josh Workman

Guitarist Josh Workman (joshworkman.com) is based out of San Francisco and still enjoys getting out on the road occasionally. His studio and tour credits include Lynda Carter, Debbie Harry, the Jazz Passengers, Larry Vuckovich, Jon Hendricks, Indigo Swing, Hot Club of San Francisco, Groove Collective, Brian Setzer, Lionel Hampton, Rosemary Clooney, and others. His commercial recording credits include work for Nintendo, Ubisoft, Apple, and various television and film productions. He also teaches privately and writes for several guitar magazines.

Essential Chord Library

G Chords

G
210003

G5
134xxx

G7
320001

C Chords

C
x32010

C5
x134xx

C7
x32410

D Chords

D
xx0132

D5
x134xx 5 fr.

D7
xx0213

Dm
xx0231

A Chords

A
x01230

A5
x012xx

A7
x02030

Am
x02310

E Chords

E
023100

E5
023xxx

E7
020100

Em
023000

B Chords

B5
x134xx

Bm
x13421

B7
x21304

F Chords

F
xx3211

F5
134xxx

Music Notation Key

The music in this book is written in standard notation and tablature. Here's how to read it.

STANDARD NOTATION

Standard notation is written on a five-line staff. Notes are written in alphabetical order from A to G.

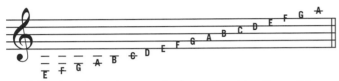

The duration of a note is determined by three things: the note head, stem, and flag. A whole note (•) equals four beats. A half note (♩) is half of that: two beats. A quarter note (♩) equals one beat, an eighth note (♪) equals half of one beat, and a 16th note (♬) is a quarter beat (there are four 16th notes per beat).

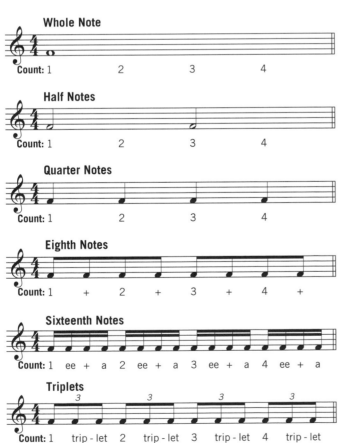

The fraction (4/4, 3/4, 6/8, etc.) or ¢ character shown at the beginning of a piece of music denotes the time signature. The top number tells you how many beats are in each measure, and the bottom number indicates the rhythmic value of each beat (4 equals a quarter note, 8 equals an eighth note, 16 equals a 16th note, and 2 equals a half note). The most common time signature is 4/4, which signifies four quarter notes per measure and is sometimes designated with the symbol ¢ (for common time). The symbol ¢ stands for cut time (2/2). Most songs are either in 4/4 or 3/4.

TABLATURE

In tablature, the six horizontal lines represent the six strings of the guitar, with the first string on the top and sixth on the bottom. The numbers refer to fret numbers on a given string. The notation and tablature in this book are designed to be used in tandem—refer to the notation to get the rhythmic information and note durations, and refer to the tablature to get the exact locations of the notes on the guitar fingerboard.

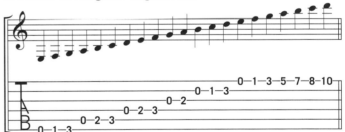

FINGERINGS

Fingerings are indicated with small numbers and letters in the notation. Fretting-hand fingering is indicated with 1 for the index finger, 2 the middle, 3 the ring, 4 the pinky, and *T* the thumb. Picking-hand fingering is indicated by *i* for the index finger, *m* the middle, *a* the ring, *c* the pinky, and *p* the thumb. Circled numbers indicate the string the note is played on. Remember that the fingerings indicated are only suggestions; if you find a different way that works better for you, use it.

PICK AND STRUM DIRECTION

In music played with a flatpick, downstrokes (toward the floor) and upstrokes (toward the ceiling) are shown as follows. Slashes in the notation and tablature indicate a strum through the previously played chord.

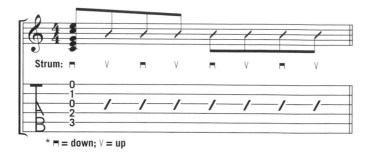

* ⊓ = **down**; ∨ = **up**

CHORD DIAGRAMS

Chord diagrams show where the fingers go on the fingerboard. Frets are shown horizontally. The thick top line represents the nut. A fret number to the right of a diagram indicates a chord played higher up the neck (in this case the top horizontal line is thin). Strings are shown as vertical lines. The line on the far left represents the sixth (lowest) string, and the line on the far right represents the first (highest) string. Dots show where the fingers go, and thick horizontal lines indicate barres. Numbers above the diagram are left-hand finger numbers, as used in standard notation. Again, the fingerings are only suggestions. An *X* indicates a string that should be muted or not played; 0 indicates an open string.

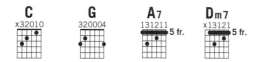

CAPOS

If a capo is used, a Roman numeral indicates the fret where the capo should be placed. The standard notation and tablature is written as if the capo were the nut of the guitar. For instance, a tune capoed anywhere up the neck and played using key-of-G chord shapes and fingerings will be written in the key of G. Likewise, open strings held down by the capo are written as open strings.

TUNINGS

Alternate guitar tunings are given from the lowest (sixth) string to the highest (first) string. For instance, D A D G B E indicates standard tuning with the bottom string dropped to D. Standard notation for songs in alternate tunings always reflects the actual pitches of the notes. Arrows underneath tuning notes indicate strings that are altered from standard tuning and whether they are tuned up or down.

VOCAL TUNES

Vocal tunes are sometimes written with a fully tabbed-out introduction and a vocal melody with chord diagrams for the rest of the piece. The tab intro is usually your indication of which strum or fingerpicking pattern to use in the rest of the piece. The melody with lyrics underneath is the melody sung by the vocalist. Occasionally, smaller notes are written with the melody to indicate the harmony part sung by another vocalist. These are not to be confused with cue notes, which are small notes that indicate melodies that vary when a section is repeated. Listen to a recording of the piece to get a feel for the guitar accompaniment and to hear the singing if you aren't skilled at reading vocal melodies.

ARTICULATIONS

There are a number of ways you can articulate a note on the guitar. Notes connected with slurs (not to be confused with ties) in the tablature or standard notation are articulated with either a hammer-on, pull-off, or slide. Lower notes slurred to higher notes are played as hammer-ons; higher notes slurred to lower notes are played as pull-offs. While it's usually obvious that slurred notes are played as hammer-ons or pull-offs, an *H* or *P* is included above the tablature as an extra reminder.

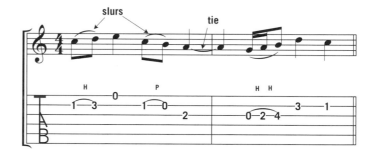

Slides are represented with a dash, and an *S* is included above the tab. A dash preceding a note represents a slide into the note from an indefinite point in the direction of the slide; a dash following a note indicates a slide off of the note to an indefinite point in the direction of the slide. For two slurred notes connected with a slide, you should pick the first note and then slide into the second.

Bends are represented with upward curves, as shown in the next example. Most bends have a specific destination pitch—the number above the bend symbol shows how much the bend raises the string's pitch: ¼ for a slight bend, ½ for a half step, 1 for a whole step.

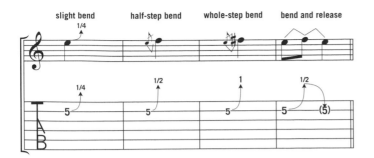

Grace notes are represented by small notes with a dash through the stem in standard notation and with small numbers in the tab. A grace note is a very quick ornament leading into a note, most commonly executed as a hammer-on, pull-off, or slide. In the first example below, pluck the note at the fifth fret on the beat, then quickly hammer onto the seventh fret. The second example is executed as a quick pull-off from the second fret to the open string. In the third example, both notes at the fifth fret are played simultaneously (even though it appears that the fifth fret, fourth string, is to be played by itself), then the seventh fret, fourth string, is quickly hammered.

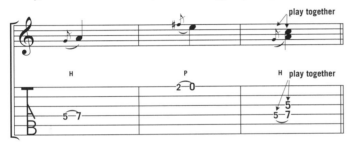

HARMONICS

Harmonics are represented by diamond-shaped notes in the standard notation and a small dot next to the tablature numbers. Natural harmonics are indicated with the text "Harmonics" or "Harm." above the tablature. Harmonics articulated with the right hand (often called artificial harmonics) include the text "R.H. Harmonics" or "R.H. Harm." above the tab. Right-hand harmonics are executed by lightly touching the harmonic node (usually 12 frets above the open string or fretted note) with the right-hand index finger and plucking the string with the thumb or ring finger or pick. For extended phrases played with right-hand harmonics, the fretted notes are shown in the tab along with instructions to touch the harmonics 12 frets above the notes.

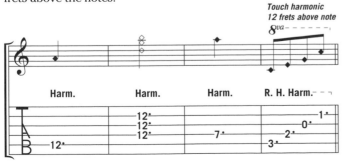

REPEATS

One of the most confusing parts of a musical score can be the navigation symbols, such as repeats, *D.S. al Coda, D.C. al Fine, To Coda*, etc. Repeat symbols are placed at the beginning and end of the passage to be repeated.

You should ignore repeat symbols with the dots on the right side the first time you encounter them; when you come to a repeat symbol with dots on the left side, jump back to the previous repeat symbol facing the opposite direction (if there is no previous symbol, go to the beginning of the piece). The next time you come to the repeat symbol, ignore it and keep going unless it includes instructions such as "Repeat three times."

A section will often have a different ending after each repeat. The example below includes a first and a second ending. Play until you hit the repeat symbol, jump back to the previous repeat symbol and play until you reach the bracketed first ending, skip the measures under the bracket and jump immediately to the second ending, and then continue.

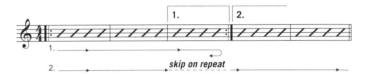

D.S. stands for *dal segno* or "from the sign." When you encounter this indication, jump immediately to the sign (𝄋). *D.S.* is usually accompanied by *al Fine* or *al Coda*. Fine indicates the end of a piece. A coda is a final passage near the end of a piece and is indicated with 𝄌. *D.S. al Coda* simply tells you to jump back to the sign and continue on until you are instructed to jump to the coda, indicated with *To Coda* 𝄌.

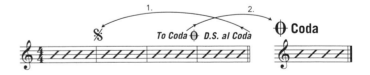

D.C. stands for *da capo* or "from the beginning." Jump to the top of the piece when you encounter this indication.

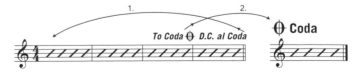

D.C. al Fine tells you to jump to the beginning of a tune and continue until you encounter the *Fine* indicating the end of the piece (ignore the *Fine* the first time through).

More Titles from String Letter Publishing

 **The Acoustic Guitar Method Complete Edition**
Book and 3 CDs
136 pp., $24.95
HL00695667

 **The Acoustic Guitar Fingerstyle Method**
Book and 2 CDs
80 pp., $24.95
HL00331948

 **The Acoustic Guitar Method Chord Book**
Book, 48 pp.,
$5.95
HL00695722

 **Rhythm Guitar Essentials**
Book and CD
71 pp., $19.95
HL00696062

 **Bluegrass Guitar Essentials**
Book and CD
72 pp., $19.95
HL00695931

 **Essential Acoustic Guitar Lessons**
Book and CD
66 pp., $19.95
HL00695802

 **Flatpicking Guitar Essentials**
Book and CD
96 pp., $19.95
HL00699174

 **Fingerstyle Guitar Essentials**
Book and CD
88 pp., $19.95
HL00699145

 **Swing Guitar Essentials**
Book and CD
80 pp., $19.95
HL00699193

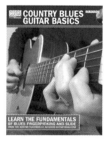 **Roots and Blues Fingerstyle Guitar**
Book and CD
96 pp., $19.95
HL00699214

 **Alternate Tunings Guitar Essentials**
Book and CD
96 pp., $19.95
HL00695557

 **Acoustic Blues Guitar Essentials**
Book and CD
72 pp., $19.95
HL00699186

 **Country Blues Guitar Basics**
Book and CD
64 pp., $19.95
HL00696222

 **Acoustic Guitar Accompaniment Basics**
Book and CD
64 pp., $14.95
HL00695430

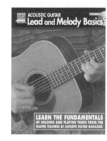 **Acoustic Guitar Solo Fingerstyle Basics**
Book and CD
64 pp., $14.95
HL00695597

 **Acoustic Guitar Chord and Harmony Basics**
Book and CD
72 pp., $16.95
HL00695611

 **Acoustic Guitar Slide Basics**
Book and CD
72 pp., $16.95
HL00695610

 **Acoustic Guitar Lead and Melody Basics**
Book and CD
64 pp., $14.95
HL00695492

FOR MORE INFORMATION, SEE YOUR LOCAL MUSIC DEALER OR WRITE TO:
Exclusively Distributed By

 **HAL•LEONARD**®

7777 W. BLUEMOUND RD. P.O. BOX 13819 MILWAUKEE, WI 53213
VISIT HAL LEONARD ONLINE AT WWW.HALLEONARD.COM